A Clear Blue Mind

Dawna Flath

BALBOA.
PRESS

A DIVISION OF HAY HOUSE

Balboa Press books may be ordered through
booksellers or by contacting:

Balboa Press
A Division of Hay House
1663 Liberty Drive
Bloomington, IN 47403
www.balboapress.com
1 (877) 407-4847

Because of the dynamic nature of the Internet, any web addresses or
links contained in this book may have changed since publication and may
no longer be valid. The views expressed in this work are solely those
of the author and do not necessarily reflect the views of the publisher,
and the publisher hereby disclaims any responsibility for them.

The author of this book does not dispense medical advice or
prescribe the use of any technique as a form of treatment for physical,
emotional, or medical problems without the advice of a physician,
either directly or indirectly. The intent of the author is only to offer
information of a general nature to help you in your quest for emotional
and spiritual well-being. In the event you use any of the information
in this book for yourself, which is your constitutional right, the author
and the publisher assume no responsibility for your actions.

Any people depicted in stock imagery provided by Thinkstock are
models, and such images are being used for illustrative purposes only.
Certain stock imagery © Thinkstock.

Print information available on the last page.

ISBN: 978-1-5043-5616-9 (sc)
ISBN: 978-1-5043-5617-6 (e)

Library of Congress Control Number: 2016906421

Balboa Press rev. date: 04/15/2016

Contents

Preface

Today, I am in a great place physically, emotionally, and spiritually. This book is the story of how I got to where I am today.

First, let me explain a little bit about the title *A Clear Blue Mind*.

Clear:
- very obvious
- not causing or allowing doubt
- easily understood
- free from doubt or confusion

Blue:
- the color of the sky and the oceans; often associated with depth and stability
- considered beneficial to the mind and body
- symbolizes trust, loyalty, wisdom, confidence, intelligence, faith, truth, and heaven

Mind:
- the part of a person that thinks, reasons, feels, and remembers
- where our soul meets our earthly being

With a clear blue mind, everything is possible.

Acknowledgments

To God and all the angels who are with me always, guiding me and giving me their love and wisdom. I have found my way because of everything you are and everything you give to me!

To my husband, Lorne, who supported me, loved me, and had faith in me every day of writing this book. I love you with all my heart and soul. Thank you!

To my son, Anthony, who was there for me every day and has taught me more than you know. I am so very proud of you and love you very much!

To my close friends, who have given me encouragement, friendship, and laughter and are always there when I need you. Thank you!

To Jeneen, thank you for guiding and supporting me through meditation and helping me to find my happiness.

To Balboa Press Publishing for helping me along the journey of publishing my first book.

Introduction

A clear blue mind is what I am working toward, and I began the journey before I even realized it—from a young girl going through her own traumas to a woman meditating and finding herself. It was during a guided meditation that I saw and spoke to my grandma, and she gave me a gift. The gift was a book, and it was blank—nothing in it. She told me that I was to write the book, and at that moment, many past memories and thoughts came together, and I realized with confidence that, yes, I was going to write a book. I was surprised at first, but then I realized that I was getting this message at exactly the right time in my life. Right at that time, my life was changing, and I was changing dramatically.

I knew in my heart and soul to trust the message to write a book. I had faith in myself to do it and faith that this was exactly what I was supposed to do. I had never entertained the thought of writing a book, and I surely didn't know *how* to write a book. But somewhere deep inside me, I just knew it was right. It was my purpose in life—or at least one of my purposes. With that knowing and faith, I sat down and asked my angels what I was supposed to write and that they guide me throughout the book. And then I just started to write.

The words just came to me from somewhere out there, or somewhere within me, or maybe it was both.

Many times, while writing this book, some of the words and ideas were new to me yet somehow familiar, as if somewhere within me, I knew all this and was just being reminded of it all.

I have put my heart, soul, and energy into this book, and I hope that these words will help everyone who is willing to stop, take a deep breath, listen, and be open to shifting their lives to see where their own highway will take them.

I ask for guidance every day to be able to see within myself and know the wisdom that is a part of my soul. I trust what I know and have faith that it will guide me to where I need to be. Every idea and thought is a small part of my wisdom, and each time I write about a new idea or thought, I get closer to seeing the bigger picture of myself and my wisdom.

If you were to journal every day about all your thoughts, ideas, experiences, dreams, and intuitions, the energy in and around you would change, along with the people around you. Your thoughts would change. The way you see people and situations would change. The way you see the world around you would change. Just acknowledging and writing down your thoughts will move you forward in your journey.

My Journey

I never thought I would be a writer, but by searching for myself, who I am, and what my purpose in life is, I have found that this is one of my purposes in life. As I write this book, I am guided by my angels. They guide me by giving me the strength, the confidence, and the words I need to write.

I have found out about myself and what my beliefs are spiritually and in this earthly life. I have learned that not only am I a powerful spiritual being, but that power has become who my earthly being is. I have found the strength to overcome anything, and that love is most powerful over everything. I have found true faith and the power that it gives us to become who we truly are.

I know that my intuition is guided by my angels, and I have learned to listen to my inner wisdom. I know they are there for me every day of my life, and I have discovered the powerful being I am, as is everyone whom God has put on this earth. I have been given guidance to true self-healing, which has led to a new chapter in my life of learning and teaching.

This is who I am, and as I write, my story comes from my soul and the words and wisdom from the angels.

Every step I take on my journey brings me closer to achieving a *clear blue mind*. With every new piece of information, expression of guidance, idea, and intuitive thought, I find my true self and what my journey is and where it is taking me.

A *clear blue mind* will give you all the wisdom you need to find yourself and take your journey with endless power and confidence.

Who Am I?

My spiritual journey began as far back as I can remember. I call it a journey because I feel that we are continually learning and following our own paths in life and searching for what is true for each of us and what makes us happy. Even though we may forget that we are on a journey, our journey still continues.

I have always had spirituality in my life. In our home when I was a child, I always felt loved and safe. Mom read us Bible stories and taught us to say our prayers. I felt safe and comforted knowing that Jesus was there for me. I remember times when I was scared, and I would sing "Jesus Loves Me." Somehow, it would make me feel protected.

I've always watched people to see how they react in situations, both good and bad, and tried to learn from them. I tried not to make mistakes that other people would make. It seemed normal for me, and I thought everyone did this. This was part of my journey, learning about others so that I would learn about myself and make my life better.

I also would lose myself in some people's energy. I would be more focused on a friend and what they wanted or would go along with their ideas, not making my own decisions or deciding what *I* wanted. I was scared to express my thoughts and ideas for fear of being made fun of. I just wanted to fit in, belong somewhere. I didn't follow my ideas or beliefs, and I did not realize that I was not learning but just following. I wasn't being who I truly was. This would take me a long time to figure out, and at least for me, I thought it was too long.

We can lose ourselves so easily, and we all have at one time or another. From a young age, we can fall into the idea of trying to fit into the right group in school, and we can lose who we truly are because we are trying to be the person we think we need to be to fit in. For the most part, my school and community were pretty cool. The only problem for me was feeling that I could not be who I truly was. I felt different and sometimes awkward around people—adults or children. It is hard to explain, but I just didn't see things the same way others did. At times, I would say something that I thought was important or I would have an idea, and the people around me wouldn't understand it. I felt dumb for thinking that way. So I usually just stayed fairly quiet and did not give my opinions. I was a follower.

Many times, I felt alone. I felt like I had to figure everything out by myself because I was different from other people. They didn't think the same way I did. I wanted to belong and feel like I fit in somewhere, just like we all do.

As a child, I felt energies around me and had this knowing, from somewhere, that something else was out there—that there was more to life than what we could physically see. At the time, I didn't understand the things I thought or felt. I am not sure how to explain what or how I felt; it was almost like feeling something is there and knowing there is more to life or about life, yet I didn't know what or where it was. It was a sense or feeling.

I wish I could tell that little girl all the things I have learned now. But I know that we all learn what we need to in our own time, and things happen when they are supposed to happen.

I would have dreams that were as real as when I was awake. From what I can remember, a lot of the dreams were scary, too. My dreams would get even more real and intense as I got older. I could even physically feel the spirits grabbing me or holding me so that I could not move.

Not all my dreams were scary. Some nights, it was more like falling into a deeper sleep that was somewhere between heaven and earth, and when I felt like I could fall even deeper, a spirit or guardian angel would call out my name very clearly and loudly. I was always annoyed by this because I felt like I was floating, I was light as air, and I felt a sense of calm that I hadn't felt before. I didn't want to come out of wherever I was. It was an amazing feeling.

As I got a little older, around high school graduation, I started to feel more confident and comfortable with who I was, and I began following my own path. This was still not easy for me. There were ups and downs, but I knew I would always figure it out. I felt a little more free to be me, but I still held back my true self. I was too scared to show who I was and have people look at me differently or think I was weird.

Family

I grew up with a grandfather who practiced massage therapy, and my mom is also a massage therapist. This seemed quite natural for me, and so I became the third generation of massage therapists in my family. Looking back at my family's history, I see many healers in my bloodline. It is interesting how our family members truly are a part of us and how similar characteristics go way back in time.

My grandpa was introduced to massage around 1955. How he became aware of massage therapy was definitely divine guidance.

Grandpa and Grandma lived on a small farm in a remote country area in central Saskatchewan. One day, a stranger came to Saskatchewan from the United States and met Grandma's brother, who introduced him to my grandpa. This stranger was looking for people who would be interested in learning how to massage. Grandpa was interested, and he began training through correspondence from Chicago.

As far as I know, this was the only place in North America at the time that taught massage therapy. I believe that this stranger was guided to Grandpa because he was meant to be a healer. Back in that day, massage was definitely not mainstream and was not understood by the medical profession or even the layperson. To be a part of something that was so new to society shows me that Grandpa had the strength and faith inside himself to know it was right and that it was a good way to help others. Grandpa is now ninety and is still practicing massage therapy today. How incredible is that?

My mom began her practice in 1982. She built her business slowly and was soon able to quit her other job and focus just on her massage practice. Many times, she would show me her study guides and anatomy books, which were very interesting. When I would massage her shoulders, she would tell me I had a very nice touch and that I was a natural. That was very encouraging to me. She is an amazing massage therapist and also continues today with her practice.

She also taught me how to be a good person, to have good manners, to share, to be kind, and to treat people with respect. I took everything I learned seriously and to heart. I was often a bit too serious. We didn't have a lot of money when I was growing up, and I took that seriously. I would never ask for anything extra. I remember one time my mom laughed at me (in a good way) because I didn't want to ask for a little change to go down to the store to buy some candy because I'd overheard her telling Dad that she had gotten a raise, but it wasn't very much. At the time, I thought it would be selfish to ask, but Mom gave me some change and told me everything would be just fine.

For some reason, when I was growing up, I took life too seriously. I had this idea in my head that I should act older, more mature. I believe this was a way for me to be taken more seriously. I have learned now that life needs to be joyful, and I take things day by day.

Take care of and provide for yourself and your family. Learn to focus on your own life and live, love, and laugh. And remember to trust that God is there to take care of you, too.

I know my dad loved all us kids, and he was a good dad. He was a truck driver, and many times during the summer, he would take one child at a time with him for the day on his truck run. I loved spending this time with him. Our summers were the most fun when we would go camping, which was every weekend from May to September and for a couple of weeks for our vacation. I can't think of a better memory than those days at the lake. I loved him, and I always felt a closeness with him. When I think back to that time and look back as an adult, I can see a glimpse of who my dad was and that he had a great spirit. His spirit would shine when he played his guitar. He taught himself to play the guitar and played different kinds of music. I lost my dad in 1984; I was thirteen.

I still remember how lonely I felt when he passed on, so I can't imagine how my mom felt. Children mourn differently than adults. I didn't know this until I was older. Children move on to their routines ... school, friends, and play. I felt guilty at first for moving on so quickly, but that is what we kids did, and it was right for us. After losing someone close to you as a child, it is very natural and important to get back to your routine. Adults can process the death of a loved one, but children don't have the experience and mature mind to deal with death the same way. At some point in their lives, when the children grow up, they will mourn that death in their own way. They will understand what it all is about and how to deal with their emotions about it.

I prefer to say someone has *crossed over* rather than using the word *died*. It may be the death of the human body, but the soul lives on, so I think it is appropriate to say *crossed over* or *passed on*.

Both of my grandmas were angels who taught me so many things. One grandma had a heart and soul that were amazingly beautiful. I believe she was a healer, too, just in a different way. She inspired people by being very patient, understanding, nonjudgmental, and spiritual, and the energy that flowed from her was peaceful. Her energy would make me feel safe and loved. It wasn't till after she crossed over that I learned that she had Jewish bloodlines in her family. She always knew, but back when she was young, she learned not to tell anyone. I wonder if this made her feel like she lost a piece of herself. How did this secret affect her? I thought it was pretty cool to learn that I had a Jewish background.

My other grandma is a very big part of my life and my family's lives. She is a pretty cool woman, loving, friendly, always there for her family. She has taught me that family is very important, and she has been there for me whenever I needed her. She was open-minded when I told her about things I saw, and she never made me feel that it was weird or wrong. I would tell her when I saw Grandpa (he had crossed over in 1979); he would be standing tall by her side, as if protecting her. I know she felt comfort in knowing that he was there for her.

I grew up with a big family around me: my parents, two sisters and a brother, grandparents, and numerous aunts, uncles, and cousins. It is really pretty cool to be close to my family.

Everyone in my family and extended family has affected my life in one way or another. No matter whether it was a good thing or a bad thing, I've learned from all the experiences I've had with them, and I am grateful to them all for everything I have learned. I know now that even in bad situations, there is something to learn, and there is something to learn from everyone in our lives—family, friends, acquaintances, or strangers.

A Day I Won't Forget

When I graduated from high school, I put the massage therapy on the back burner. I wanted to go out and work and take life from there. I moved from home and waitressed, which I was good at, and I had a good job at a nice restaurant. I had two really good roommates, and they are still my friends today. When I look back, I wish I could have been more open with them. We always got along and we had fun together, but I think I always had a bit of a wall up, trying to protect myself. I was emotionally struggling with my secrets and too scared to deal with them. I always tried to do my best, and I hope, after reading my book, my friends will see another part of who I am.

It was like I forgot who I truly was. I felt confused, scared, and a little angry. I was trying to fix something inside me. Something was not right, and I knew what it was, but I really was trying to forget about it. Even as I write about it now, my stomach turns to knots. It makes me feel nervous and ill, so I guess I still have some emotions to work on.

All of these emotions come from my being raped. I struggled emotionally with this for a very long time. It was hard to manage by myself, but I felt like I had to. Again, I told myself it would be okay and that I would figure it out. This is what happened:

It was 1989, and I was staying with friends. One night, we went to a bar. I didn't have much money back then, only enough to buy a drink or two. My friends went off somewhere in the bar, and I sat at a table by myself. A guy came up to my table and offered to buy me a drink. I said yes,and that was the beginning of a very scary night. Back then, I hadn't heard of the date rape drug, but that is what happened that night. I still tear up when I relive it. My friends said they saw me leave the bar with someone that night, early in the evening, and so when they went to leave and didn't see me, they just left, not realizing what was going on.

I didn't know I had left the bar that night. When I came to, I was in the bar's washroom after it had closed. The employees were still there, and one of them gave me a ride. My whole body felt dirty. I was so embarrassed. I knew I had been raped; I just didn't understand how I lost the memory of the entire night. I was so embarrassed to talk to the employees and ask for a ride. I was scared, alone, confused, and embarrassed that I didn't know what exactly had happened to tell anyone. I felt as though my spirit had dropped out of me. The hurt sank so deep that it felt like it broke my soul. How does someone do this to another person? I never understood how people can treat others this way.

It was very confusing to hear my friends say that I had left with someone that night, because that isn't something I would have done, so it upset me to hear that. I felt so alone and scared at the thought of what all could have happened that night. I was also confused about how I could have no memory of what had happened. How was I raped without some memory of it?

I tried very hard to forget it and even tried to convince myself that it hadn't happened at all. After a while, I had pushed the memory way back in my mind, but I still had emotions to deal with. Even though we can make ourselves forget a trauma in our lives, our personality, the spirit of who we are, and our energy changes. Some people become angry, withdrawn, or quiet, or they change any way that the person can just to manage. I felt like I lost myself. I felt sad and alone. I turned my emotions inside and told no one.

I had been married for a few years when I first heard about the date rape drug. I knew right away that it was what the guy in the bar had used. The emotions all came flooding back, and again I tried to ignore them. I knew it was time to confide in my husband, but I was so very nervous to tell him. It was an embarrassing thing for me to talk about, but he was understanding and supportive. Talking about it helped a little, but I had a long journey of healing ahead of me. I still didn't think about finding any help—like therapy. For some reason, I thought I should be able to deal with it on my own. I just had to find the right way to heal from this.

Marriage

Lorne and I knew each other in high school but didn't date until after I graduated. We share the same birthday, but he is two years older. We dated for about a year and a half and then were married in 1991. We were both pretty young, but it truly felt *right*. Every cell in my body just knew it was right. If you have ever felt that sense of truth within you, it is really cool to feel that knowing. We learned to grow with each other, and we learned to grow individually. I think it is important to learn to be a couple, to be united, and to share your lives with each other. To be able to share everything strengthens the bond and trust between you. If you have respect, patience, and love and listen to each other, your marriage can make it through anything. Have fun, laugh, and support each other always.

We have been married twenty-five years in July 2016 and have raised our son, Anthony. Anthony has wanted to be a farmer since he started to walk and talk, and he now works with us on our family farm.

Marriage definitely has ups and downs. We have always worked through the stressful times, even when it got really hard and it was difficult to see the light on the other side. We always managed to figure it out and become closer to each other, every time. We always loved each other and always remembered that love when we went through stressful times.

If you work at your marriage with everything you have, it will just get better. It is worth all the energy you put into it. We have an amazing marriage that just gets better and better. We both have our own paths in life, and we help each other out along the way. Over the years, we have learned about who we are, individually and as a couple. We support each other in every way, and I am so thankful for my husband and family.

My Massage Practice

In 1991 I started my massage practice. I had learned to listen to a client's body through my hands. I could listen by touch, and my hands knew exactly what needed to be done. If I tried too hard to think of what I should do, I would not listen to my instincts. Sometimes our lives get so busy or stressful that we forget to just take a breath and relax. I would always try to do the best that I could. I learned to trust my hands and my instincts, and later realized that this was just the beginning of my learning and having faith in how I worked.

Over the years, I attended many different classes to maintain my massage license. Every class I took opened my mind even further to how the body worked and the possibilities of how the body could heal. I have always said that the most important lesson I have learned is that the more I learn about the human body, the more I realize how much I don't know. Our bodies are amazingly complicated, and each one of us is unique.

When I began attending craniosacral therapy classes through the Upledger Institute in 2000, I knew right away that this was what I needed to do in my practice. The Upledger Institute describes craniosacral therapy as "a light-touch approach that releases tensions deep in the body to relieve pain and dysfunction and improve whole-body health and performance." Our bodies hold tension, stress, and emotional and physical traumas. We listen with our hands and monitor the rhythm of the fluid that is flowing around your central nervous system. We can find weak fluid movement or muscle motion, and this guides us to where we need to work on the body. This therapy can release the tissue memory of all these problems and allow the body to heal. I would integrate this therapy with my massage or use it on its own. I loved the fact that it not only focused on the physical body but also the emotional and spiritual part of who we are. I became more aware of the inner physician, the spirituality, and how truly powerful we are.

We are spiritual beings, and so it is natural for the spiritual being to come forth and be a part of the healing. Our spiritual being knows what we need. We just have to listen to connect with that soul. It is our instinct and that sense of knowing that the soul communicates with us. I was opened up to a whole new way of healing.

Believing Is Wisdom

The words "believing is wisdom" came to me while I was praying. I was having a bit of a down day, and when I feel like this, I always make a point to remind myself that I choose to be happy, and I change my thoughts to positive ones. I felt like I needed to pray for guidance. I heard words resonating in me that I needed to believe not only in the power of God and the angels that he sends to us, but to believe in myself, in who I am and how powerful I am.

I always have music playing in my home all day long, and on that day, I had a '70s music channel playing. While I was praying and asking for guidance, the song "The Lord's Prayer" came on. I didn't know anyone had ever made it into a song, but there it was as I prayed. It was a very cool experience. I continued my prayer, and right after "The Lord's Prayer," they played a song called "Heaven Is on the Seventh Floor." Again, I had never heard this song, but these two songs were a huge validation of my prayer being heard and answered!

I knew that in order to believe, I just had to let go of myself and let God take over. I had to question the depth of my belief. It made me realize that no matter how much I believed in what God can do and what I could truly be and do, it was far from what God can really do and how powerful he has made all of us. I am learning very quickly that the possibilities are endless. I am so thankful to all the people around the world who share their amazing stories and miracles, because they help us to keep on *believing*! The more I let go, the more I hear and see the powerful spiritual beings around me, and by believing in them, I can ask for guidance and receive their words of wisdom.

If we keep an open mind to all possibilities, it's amazing how much we can learn. We don't have to agree with or believe in everything we hear or read, but if we are open to other ideas, we can trust our own instincts and always know what is right for us and find what our beliefs are. The world is filled with amazing people with amazing information. Just be open to learning and "be who you be."

Bringing the craniosacral therapy to my practice was harder than I thought it would be. It was new to society and so took time to understand and accept. I also had a hard time incorporating it into the practice because it was different. It deals with emotions and spirituality, which most people have a hard time dealing with. It's human nature to want to take the easy way and not deal with problems in their lives. That can hold us back from learning about who we are and about life. If you face your struggles, emotions, or situation head on and deal with it, you will find it really wasn't that hard or scary. And you will see how much more joy is in your life.

I had to have faith in the therapy and in myself, too, or it just wouldn't work. If the client has no belief or trust in the therapy, it just doesn't affect them as much as it could. Not believing in the therapy blocks the energy of the healing because the client is unwilling to receive it. So it is important to have an open mind to all things. I had to learn to trust my instincts, what I felt and what I saw. It can be difficult to change what we have been taught, but if we are open to learn something new, then we can make up our own minds. It is our choice either to live only with what we have been taught or to keep learning and find our own beliefs. We tend to fear the unknown, but if you can keep an open mind and learn about something new, you can then decide how you feel about it.

The more I worked with craniosacral therapy, the more it became natural. I learned to listen, to trust my instincts, and I found how spiritual healing truly is. I became more aware of my guardian angels and how they help me every day. I felt comfort in knowing that I just needed to ask them and they would be there for me.

One time that sticks in my memory is a day I was driving on very snowy and icy roads. I was by myself and getting very scared, so I prayed that my guardian angels would keep me safe. It was the coolest thing: I could feel and see an angel sitting on my shoulder and another angel behind me. Although the drive was still a little unnerving, I felt protected and safe. This was one of the first times I saw the angels around me, and it would only get more interesting after that.

I continued to ask my guardian angels or spiritual guides to be with me, whether it was while I was working, driving, or stressed, or I just wanted their comforting presence around me. If you ask your guardian angels to be with you, they will be there in a heartbeat. That's their job, and they love to be there to help. You just have to ask.

My Dad and My Nephew

The first time I saw my dad's spirit was while I was working on a client at home. I looked up from the client, and there he was, sitting in the corner of the massage room! My first reaction was that it couldn't be right that I could see him. Why would I see him? And why now? Then I realized that I see my angels and spiritual guides, so why not my dad's spirit? It was a great feeling. I hadn't seen him since I was thirteen, and it was comforting that he was there for me.

My nephew would come to our house often, whether it was for the day, overnight, or for a longer period of time during summer holidays. He crossed over at the age of three and a half. He was born with vein of Galen malformation, which is abnormal connections between arteries and deep-draining veins of the brain. The capillaries, which normally connect arteries to veins and function to slow blood flow, allowing for the drop-off of oxygen and nutrients to the brain, are missing. It is a rare condition. After he had procedures to fix them, he was a normal little guy. Then he started to get sick, and we all thought it was a cold, but it wouldn't go away. He became very sick and was sent back to Toronto to the doctor who had done the procedures to fix his vein of Galen malformation. There were no problems with those veins, so they started to look elsewhere. The doctor found an even rarer medical condition in his liver. They called it a liver fistula. His blood had totally bypassed his liver, so it had never been cleaned, and the liver never performed all the vital functions that it needed to do for the blood.

My sister and brother-in-law were at the hospital in another province. We got a phone call early in the morning that it wouldn't be long before he was gone. My mom, my niece, and I flew out that day to try to get to the children's hospital in Toronto before he crossed over. We didn't make it, but we got to see him and say goodbye.

After that, I understood when someone would say, "It hurts so bad that you feel like you're going to die." My body literally felt like it was dying, so I can't even imagine what my sister and brother-in-law were feeling.

Back at the hotel the next day, my sister was asleep on one bed and my mom asleep on the other. My brother-in-law and niece were across the hall in another room with more family. I had gone down to the snack bar in the hotel and picked up some food in case someone was hungry back in the room. I was a bit annoyed at first because everything there seemed strawberry-themed: strawberry muffins, strawberry jams, that kind of thing. I like strawberries, but not that much. Later, I told my sister about everything being strawberry-flavored at the snack bar, and she told me that my nephew had loved strawberries. I guess that was my nephew's way of saying that he was there.

When I got back to the room, I sat in the corner that faced the door and tried to eat something, and all of a sudden, there they were! Standing in front of the door in the room, my dad and my nephew! I was shocked at first, and in disbelief. They stood there as I stared at them. I looked over to my sister and mom, but they were both still sleeping. I needed to make sure I was actually seeing what I was seeing ... to make sure they were truly there. So I asked my nephew to walk over and touch his mom's foot. (Tears come to my eyes as I write this.) He walked over and held his mom's foot, and as he did this, my sister's foot began to move slowly back and forth. I was still kind of shocked, but so very thankful to see him and to know that our dad had been there for his grandson when he crossed over.

I knew this was my dad's and nephew's way of sending the message that he was okay and with family. They didn't say anything to me, yet I knew exactly what they were telling me without words. I didn't say anything to my sister and brother-in-law until we were on the plane, on the way home. They were both surprised and I think a little comforted knowing that their son was okay and with his grandpa. They needed to know what I saw and that their son was happy and with family.

Depression and Decisions

I struggled with depression for a while. This was a very low time in life that began when I took a prescription to quit smoking. I had smoked cigarettes for twenty years. At first, I didn't realize that I was changing. Over about five or six weeks of taking the prescription, depression slowly took hold, and by the time I realized what was going on, I was a very different person. I had changed tremendously.

One day, I realized that not only was I not happy, but I wasn't thinking the same way I normally did. I couldn't think positive thoughts no matter how much I tried; they always came out negatively. I found I couldn't handle any kind of stress the way I used to. Before this, I could handle anything, help anyone, and deal with any stress that came my way. I could help people just by being there to listen or to help solve a problem. The negativity of situations or people wouldn't bother me; I could handle it. I was pretty laid back and easygoing and always tried to find the positive in everything. But now I was a totally different person.

My family and I were also dealing with a loss in our family and the stress of the fallout from that loss. This pushed me to my limit. I was on antidepressants, but I still had a very hard time dealing with it all. If God was testing me to see how much I could handle, then I had had enough. I didn't know how much more stress I could handle. I prayed to God and told him I had had enough. It was amazing how I found more strength to handle any stress that came my way.

I knew I had to deal with whatever came my way, and deep down I knew I could get through it all. I prayed a lot for help and guidance. There were days when I didn't know my purpose in this life or why God would give me so much to deal with. I didn't feel well physically or emotionally, and I was struggling to deal with the business side of the family's loss. During this depression, I truly understood why some people take their own lives. You can't control your thoughts or your feelings. I had days I had to force myself to have a positive thought. This might be hard to understand if you have never experienced it, but it sure taught me the power of the mind and how it can change and control our lives. Through the bad days, I knew what was right, and I knew that any negative thoughts weren't who I truly was, so I kept reminding myself that it wasn't me, that everything would be okay, and that I would get through it.

My family and I did get through it all with a lot of hard work and *a lot of faith!* I put my trust in faith, knowing it was right. Something inside told me that it was all going to be all right, so I followed my instincts. I was eventually able to stop taking the antidepressants, which was a great relief. I believe our bodies can heal from anything. There are so many stories of people from all over the world who have healed from many different things.

From there, I started to make decisions to change my life and make it better. I knew through the years that I didn't feel happy. I began to pay attention to the little thoughts of wondering, *Why don't I feel happiness?* The feeling of sadness got stronger over time, and I finally realized that if I didn't deal with what was making me sad and literally sick, it would continue to eat away at me and my soul. I had to be honest with myself and figure out what was going on with me. A part of me knew that practicing massage therapy was not making me happy anymore, and I had considered giving it up, but I always pushed those thoughts out of my mind. It was too scary to think of leaving my clients and not having that income. I had gotten quite sick, and I tried many different avenues to find out what was wrong with me. I knew how I felt, but no one understood what I was telling them. I felt as though I didn't have stomach acid, so that when I ate, the food wasn't digesting.

This went on for at least a year, and maybe more. I had gained weight, and I would go days without eating because I felt so terrible. And when I did eat, I would only eat tuna from a can and Rice Krispies, because these foods caused the least pain. I finally talked to a naturopathic doctor, and he agreed to let me try hydrochloric acid pills when I ate.

Wow! What a difference! My body could now digest food properly, and I felt so good. Once I began the pills and started to digest, the weight came off naturally, the stomach pain abated, and a lot of the joint and body pain disappeared.

I still had some issues, so we did food allergy tests and found out that I had many food allergies. It made perfect sense: with my body not digesting food for so long, practically everything I had eaten had become foreign to my body, so my body developed allergies to those foods. After finding this out, I made sure to be careful what I ate.

I began to feel normal again, but still had physical pain and was always exhausted. After about two years, I was diagnosed with fibromyalgia.

I still could not admit to myself that I needed to leave the massage practice behind me, so I continued to practice massage but cut down on my days. This helped a bit. I kept trying to figure out what I needed to do to make myself well again. I knew my body could heal; I just had to figure out how to do it. I knew I had to work on emotional traumas in my life, and I had to be brutally honest with myself. No more fooling myself and hiding from emotions and the past. I thought I could work on all of this myself, and I did have a good start and dealt with some of things I needed to, but asking for help is a great thing!

A friend took me to an Access Consciousness Bars energy class, and from that moment on, I "got it"! Everything, including what I needed to do, was clear to me. I met the person who I knew would help. I knew that all I had to do was ask, and I emailed her the day after the class. I am so thankful for the friend who introduced me to this new way of healing and for the women who instructed that first class—they are spiritually beautiful women, and I am grateful for their first class!

One big lesson that I learned from the Access Consciousness class was to "be who I be." I loved the way they said it—"be who you be." It makes you take notice and pay attention to the words. I had known deep down that I needed to be myself, but I didn't truly get it until that class. I had been hiding who I truly was, and I needed to be me, no matter what anyone else thought of it.

It doesn't matter what others may think of you; that's their opinion, and they have the right to it, just like you have the right to your own opinion. But please be mindful of not judging others. Judging others is a negative energy that can consume us. It is important to keep positive thoughts and focus on your own life and what you and your family need, not on everyone else's business. That's not yours to judge or focus on. Like I have heard Oprah say: "Stay in your own lane." I love this phrase, how better can it be said?

Sometimes we hear or read something that we think we "get" but actually we don't. We truly didn't "get it," and we don't even realize until later what the lesson was. It can pop into our heads out of nowhere, and then we "get it."

My first step to finding myself, my purpose, and true happiness was to be honest with myself about all my emotions and thoughts. This was one of the hardest things I have ever done. The amount of energy used to hold on to traumas, or whatever it is you are holding on to, is a huge amount. Holding on to these negative feelings will exhaust you physically and emotionally.

I realized that being a massage therapist wasn't who I was anymore. It was a huge part of my life, and I learned so much from it, but it was time to move on. I made the decision to stop practicing massage therapy and focus on a new energy therapy. It was scary at first, but I knew in my heart that it was right for me. And when I put my faith in trusting what is right for me, it really is pretty amazing— not that scary at all. I actually felt relieved and happier. I was back on my path; my journey had started moving forward again. When we forget about following our path, our journey sits on that path, waiting for us to jump back in and start moving again.

I realized the stomach problems and the fibromyalgia had come into my life because of emotional traumas and that I was not being who I truly was.

After emailing the instructor from the Access Consciousness class, we had a great session. I acknowledged and let go of so many things that I had hidden for so many years. I felt free and light by admitting and letting go of traumas that I had been through. It was terrifying and amazing at the same time. It was terrifying at first to say these things out loud, but I felt absolutely amazing after I let it all out. I began healing physically and emotionally that day. I felt like a whole new person, and I actually could feel joy deep inside me that flowed through my body and out to the universe.

During that first class, the instructors worked with all of us at the same time. Different people had different situations or emotions that the instructors would pick up on and then help them let go of. At one point, the lady who would later work privately with me picked up a book, opened it to a random page, and then read the page. She asked which of us this topic related to. I knew it was me, but I couldn't bring myself to admit it, since my good friend was beside me and she had no idea of this part of my past. The instructor waited a minute and then just let the topic go and moved on to something else. The page she read was about a man who had been sexually assaulted when he was a young boy. This was my story, too. I just couldn't admit it in front of my friend. I finished the class, and when I returned home, I called the instructor and asked to have a private session with her.

Later, when I had a session with the instructor, I told her that the page she read in class was about me. She said that she knew she had been drawn to that particular page for a reason. This was a huge step for me to relive, as much as I could remember, and go through the emotions of that very terrible and lonely time. I was only about nine or ten when it happened. I didn't understand what was going on; it was very confusing. I didn't know what to do or why it was happening. I was so scared, embarrassed, and lonely. When I go back to that time, I still feel all the emotions I felt then. I didn't want to relive those feelings, but I knew I would be okay and feel stronger for doing it. The innocence of my childhood left that day, and I never felt the same. I lost a piece of who I was, and my spirit was broken. I didn't feel joy or laughter much after that. Even as an adult, it would almost surprise me when I would start truly laughing, and it felt joyful inside my heart. It was rare that I would laugh and actually feel joy, true joy.

I never told anyone. Not my dad, my mom, no one. It was too scary and embarrassing. When I did start to deal with the abuse, I told my husband, and it wasn't as hard as I thought it would be. We have to work on overcoming our fears because when we push through the fear, we realize that on the other side of that fear, it really isn't that bad, and the fear isn't that scary to let go of. Letting go of my fear gave me even more joy in my life! When you get rid of the negative energy in your body, it leaves much more room for the positive energy and joy. I not only asked the instructor for help, but I also asked God and my guardian angels to be there for me and guide and protect me as I worked on making my life better.

It's been a long time of healing, emotionally and physically, but I feel amazing! Even the physical problems are healing. The fibromyalgia is getting better all the time, and my body is healing the food allergies, too. I can now eat without problems some of the foods that had caused allergic reactions before, and though others still give me trouble, my body's reactions are not as severe as they once were.

So many people struggle with all kinds of things in their lives, and I hope they know they are not alone. Everyone is important and deserves to have a happy, joyful life. Just look for the right kind of therapy and the right people who will help you find your way to happiness. Ask your guardian angels to help guide you to the right place and to people who will help you. Trust your instincts when you do find the right person. Your inner guide knows all, so trust that feeling. It never hurts to try something new, you may find a whole new way to look at yourself and life.

Something I do when I am looking for an answer about something is go to a bookstore and ask my guardian angels to guide me to a book that will help me find my answer. It works amazingly well! The more you listen to your instincts, inner guide, or guardian angels, the easier it gets. Just have faith and trust in yourself. I have heard stories of all sorts of people overcoming all kinds of traumas, unthinkable situations, medical problems, and just about anything. I know everyone can overcome their difficult life situations too! It's your choice to dig down deep and deal with whatever it is you need to let go of. I finally made my choice to jump in and do it, no matter how hard it was, and you can, too. Just choose to take control of your life.

Making the decision to take control of my life and go out and look for the help and answers I needed got me back in my lane and moving forward. This is my mystic highway, though finding out who I truly am and what my purpose is has been difficult, emotionally draining, fearful, insightful, fun, joyful, and crazy amazing. I am still learning and finding my way down my life path. It's like the John Fogerty song "Mystic Highway." What a beautiful song of letting a mystical highway lead you to the next part of your journey. I love this analogy of your life path. When I first heard this song, I knew that was exactly how I felt. I was on my mystic highway, and it was taking me to all kinds of places, physically and spiritually.

Sometimes, when we lose focus on our lives and who we are, we find that our journey along the mystic highway has come to a halt. When we are more focused on other people's lives, or maybe lost in depression, we will sit alongside the mystic highway and watch all the other people pass by on their journeys. So remind yourself daily to stay with your own journey. Don't worry about your neighbor's journey. When we "be who we be," we are happier and more content, and this will show through to our family and friends. Life all around us will be more joyful, fun, and full of love. You just never know where your mystic highway will take you, so get back in the driver's seat of your life and follow your mystic highway.

We all know what we believe in, even if we think we don't know. Our souls know all, including who we are. If you feel that something is true to you, then it probably is right for you. We are all different, so everyone's truth is different. Our beliefs are all different, and that is fine because we are all unique. We don't have to be like everyone else; just "be who you be." Don't judge someone else for their beliefs or yourself for your own. If someone judges you, that is their problem, not yours. They have lost their way or are sitting along their mystic highway, stalled, too busy in other people's lives or in the material world to live their own life.

If we can all find who we truly are and follow our purpose in life, we will all be happier and enjoy a more joyful life on earth. In the end, it all comes down to the same thing: A joyful, happy life full of spirituality and love. If we can manage this, not only will we heal our lives physically, emotionally, and spiritually, but we will also help heal the earth. The earth gives us everything we need, and we must keep it healthy. The earth is a part of us all and a reflection of who we are. The earth can inspire our spiritual being and feed and nurture our human being.

Meditation

I have found great peace and contentment in practicing meditation. Years ago, when I first began trying meditation, I found it difficult, but I would try especially when I was stressed.

The best explanation of meditation is from Yoga International. They explain meditation as "a precise technique for resting the mind and attaining a state of consciousness that is totally different from the normal waking state. It is the means for fathoming all the levels of ourselves and finally experiencing the center of consciousness within." Yoga International also says, "Meditation is not a part of any religion; it is a science, which means that the process of meditation follows a particular order, has definite principles, and produces results that can be verified. In meditation, the mind is clear, relaxed, and inwardly focused. When you meditate, you are fully awake and alert, but your mind is not focused on the external world or on the events taking place around you." Calming our minds is a great way to relieve stress and is wonderful for helping you heal physically or emotionally. There are many ways to meditate, and your state of mind can deepen the more you practice. Meditation is a very important part of my life.

When I had the chance to have a guided meditation, I was very excited. This meditation is instructed by a trained practitioner or teacher. They guide you through the meditation and help you to understand events, situations, or symbols in your meditation. I don't know why I was excited, since my meditations at home were more calming than exciting. Maybe it was because I had started a new part of my life and I was very excited about where my journey was taking me.

The meditation was guided by Jeneen, one of the women I took my first Access Consciousness class with. There were six of us in the meditation. I knew no one there, which normally would make me quiet and feel shy, but that night, I felt confident and I enjoyed meeting them all. I knew I was there for me and my journey; the others were there for their own reasons. The confidence felt good because I was usually worried about what others would think of me. We all can feel protective of ourselves, of what we say or what we do, because we are afraid of being judged, being laughed at.

I have learned that it is okay to be me, and if someone is going to judge, that is their problem, not mine. Feeling confident, I knew that when we began the meditation, I could open up my mind to all possibilities and allow my mind and body to relax and receive whatever was going to happen. Jeneen took us to the most wonderful and vivid places in our meditation. At one stop along our journey was a rocky shore, and just beyond that was a cave. In my journey, my grandma, who had passed away a few years before, was there waiting for me! Everything was so very real! I walked over to her, knelt down, and hugged her. She held me, and the feeling was so amazing, I cried. She looked younger, but I felt the comforting energy that she had always had. Her love surrounded me.

It is almost indescribable. It's a calming, peaceful feeling yet exciting at the same time. I can still feel what I felt during that meditation, but I am having a hard time putting it into words. My grandma is one of my spiritual guides. That is quite fitting for her, since she always was very spiritual.

Then Jeneen guided all the meditators to ask whomever they had met on their meditation if they had anything to give. I asked my grandma if she had anything for me. She handed me a large book. It was blank—nothing on the cover or in the book. I thanked her for it and continued on my journey.

After the meditation was over, Jeneen asked us to write down everything we could remember about the journey. She then asked us to talk about our journey with the rest of the group. Normally, I would have been nervous to speak in front of strangers, let alone talk about such a personal event, but I was the first to volunteer. Jeneen took me through the journey from beginning to end and explained what everything meant and symbolized. When she asked me what my guide had given me, I hesitated at first because I thought maybe I hadn't seen it right or something. I told her that my grandma had handed me a book, but that it was completely blank. Right away, Jeneen said, "Oh, you are going to write a book."

I was speechless! I knew right then that, yes, I was going to write a book.

Before this guided meditation, I had no thoughts, urges, or desires to write a book, but when she told me that's what it meant, I flashed back to a few different times in my life when an inner voice told me to write a book. I hadn't heard this voice for quite some time, but, wow, was this ever a clear message. This voice told me to write a book a few times over the years, and I was standing in the same place in my house every time I heard it. And whenever I did, I would first wonder where the voice was coming from, but then I would say to myself, "Yeah, right! Write a book. I don't think so." What on earth would I write about? And I'm not a writer. I have no idea how to write a book! Well here I am … writing a book. Funny how life can change so quickly.

I continue doing meditation at home on my own, and I find it much easier to focus, relax, listen, and trust what I see and hear. It is interesting that most of my meditations last the same amount of time: forty-five minutes. Maybe this means something, I am not sure, but I am still learning so much and loving every moment. I ask every day for my spiritual guides to be with me and guide me, especially while writing this book.

When I started writing, I was a little nervous, but I asked my spiritual guides to guide me while I wrote, and I actually feel pretty at ease writing. Even when I sit down to write, and I have no idea what I am going to write that day. I ask for their guidance and I just start writing. How cool is that? I am so thankful for their presence and guidance.

Acknowledging our thoughts and ideas is very important. Many times, these thoughts or ideas are from our spiritual guides, guardian angels, or intuition—if that is what you call it. Everyone has his or her own beliefs, and what is right for one person may not be for the next person. I believe in God, spiritual guides, angels, earth angels, and so much more. I keep an open mind in whatever I learn, hear, or see. I know what is right and is the truth for me. When I have a heavy or uncomfortable feeling, then I know it isn't right or the truth for me.

If we acknowledge the thoughts and ideas we have, it guides us down our journey in life. We just need to listen. Often, our egos get in the way, or we are so busy with life that we don't hear or see the information that is given to us. Our egos are created from our fears, so if your thoughts are negative and telling you, for example, that you can't do something or you are not good enough, then this is definitely your ego talking. We are all powerful, infinite beings who can do anything we put our minds to. Every time your ego tries to take over, just ask it to keep its thoughts to itself. Trust your instincts, that feeling inside you to be who you be. You are never alone, so ask your guardians to help and support you through tough times.

Angel Help

I have asked my guardian angels and archangels for help many times. One situation that I didn't know how to fix was after my nephew crossed over and my sister was devastated. I wanted to support her in the best way I could. She seemed to become stuck in her overwhelming grief. I had spent every day with her for about a month. She would call me every morning to make sure I was coming to see her.

For the first couple of weeks, I stopped seeing my massage clients, but too much time was passing, and I needed to get back to work. I started to take clients in the early morning so I could be done before my sister called. I was tired. I tried to take care of my family, my business, and my sister. I didn't know how to tell her that I couldn't be with her all the time. She lost her little boy, and how could I not support her?

After about a month or so, I picked up one of Doreen Virtue's books and read about archangels and how they can help us if we just ask. She talked about how each archangel could help us in different situations. I read about Archangel Michael and how he can protect us. When someone is attached to you energetically and they are looking for support or they become too needy, they don't realize they are stuck in this place of needing constant support and giving up their control of their life.

They can't move on, and it will hold you back, too. So that night when I went to bed, I asked Archangel Michael to help me break this attachment that was holding my sister back from healing and help guide her through this difficult time in her life.

Following Doreen's advice, I visualized a cord that attached me to my sister. Then I visualized cutting that cord and releasing both of us. At first, it felt as though I would be cutting the bond that we had as sisters, but I knew that bond would last forever, and it was the unhealthy attachment that was being released. It was the right thing to do. As soon as I cut the cord between us, I felt lighter. I knew that our bond as sisters would always be there, but the attachment she created was not healthy and was stopping her from healing from the loss of her son.

The next day definitely confirmed that it had worked! That fast!

My sister called me, like she did every morning, but this time her voice seemed a little lighter, and she wanted to come to my house instead of me going to her. I knew right away that something had shifted inside her. That whole day she was more talkative, helped me make meals, and was just different somehow. I could see that she was beginning to heal.

I am so thankful for Archangel Michael that he is there whenever we ask him for help. I am also thankful for Doreen Virtue and her books that I find so helpful.

Taking our own journeys through life, down that mystic highway, we all travel at our own pace. It's our individual journey, so it is only right to go at our own pace. We all have much to learn, and it is different for each of us. We will learn the lessons that we are supposed to when we are ready for them. Have faith in yourself, listen to your intuition, and ask your guardian angels or spiritual guides for help. If we ask for guidance, we find our way with more ease. Our angels or guides send us messages all the time, and we may hear it as a thought, or maybe we see something on TV that gives us an idea or is intriguing enough to catch our attention. Many messages that I get are words or phrases that I hear continuously, and when I pay attention to them, I usually understand what they mean right away. Sometimes it takes me a while to figure out what the message means. I often have memories or just a thought of someone who has passed or an angel, and it is constant until I acknowledge the thought or memory and realize those who have passed and the angels are right there with me. If you listen more to your thoughts, you will be surprised how many you just let float by your consciousness. Angels give us messages in many ways, so when something catches your attention, take a moment to acknowledge it. It may be an answer that you are looking for.

A great example of getting a message and not seeing it is when I found *The Hiding Place*. It had pleasantly surprised me spiritually. When I moved in to my husband's home, which had been the farm house he grew up in, I found a book that his mom had left there. I was cleaning one day and found the book in a closet. I had never heard of the book, and at the time, I had no urge to read it. Without thinking, I just put it away. I could have given it away, since I didn't really have any interest in it, but I kept it without giving it a second thought. I would forget about the book but would find it from time to time over the next six or seven years, and I always just put it away again. The last time I found the book, without thinking about what I was doing, I put it in one of the end tables in the living room, and shortly after that, I picked it up and started reading it.

The book was *The Hiding Place* by Corrie ten Boom. It is about a family who was caught hiding Jews in their home during World War II and then sent to concentration camps. I loved it! It was so amazing to get to know this family and their journey through such a terrible time. They were thankful for what they had even though they were in a concentration camp and had nothing. Corrie's sister showed her how even being thankful for the lice was good: The Nazi soldiers would not come around them because of the lice, so this was a good thing, and they thanked God for the lice. I learned so much from Corrie and her family, and I am very thankful for each of them. Not only was their story amazing, but their spiritual journey was truly incredible, and it opened up my spirituality and faith in God even more.

I know my angels guided me to that book over the years, and when I was finally ready, I took notice of it and read the book. I know that if I had read that book when I first found it years earlier, it wouldn't have affected me the way it did. Somehow, I knew it was time to read it, and so did the angels who guided me to the book. Thank you to my angels for continuing to guide me.

Our lives will have happy, joyful times, and we will also have struggles, hardships, and times when we don't know how we will go on. If we just have faith, like the ten Booms, then the hard times will be less scary, hurtful, and confusing. There are so many stories of amazing people and how they get through unthinkable situations or overcome physical and mental trauma that we can learn from, if we just take the time and are willing to learn from others.

You may even find someday that someone has learned something from you. Quite often, we help others without realizing we have done so. Maybe we said just the right words at the right time for someone who needed to hear those words. Maybe we did something that we thought was small and insignificant, but someone else saw it and it changed their lives. A simple smile and "good morning" or "hello" to a stranger can change their day, and maybe they will give that happiness to everyone they meet that day. It can be that easy. It is pretty cool.

My Experiment

Years ago, I used to experiment with the concept of simple interactions with people. It was interesting to watch people's reactions and how they changed every time I saw them. I am from a small town, and I got to know most people in the community. The ones I didn't know well, I at least knew their names, or their faces were familiar to me. So when I drove through town and passed people I didn't know, I would smile and wave to them. It was interesting to see their reactions the first time I would wave to them. They would give me that look of "why are you waving at me when I don't even know you?" It was funny to watch their reactions. Then I would see them again another day and smile and wave to them again. By the second or third time, they would be smiling and waving back to me. It was such a cool feeling. They went from being so-called strangers to a friend. And who knows? Maybe they passed on that feeling of happiness to others. That would be cool!

Another thing I learned through my massage and cranial work was the power of touch, and I thought it would be fun to try the power of touch when I worked in a store. I decided to make a point of touching the customers' hands when I gave them their change, and I always held the intention of kindness. I did this to everyone every time they came to the store. It was amazing how people change over a short time. My hand touching their hands while giving them their change was enough to actually affect them. My energy connected to their energy. When we hold the intention of kindness or love during our day, that energy will not only surround us but it will touch others around us.

Just keeping your intentions of love or kindness and having positive thoughts will help you see your life in a new way. Your stresses won't seem as difficult to deal with. The people around you will change for the better, too. Life can seem so dramatic sometimes, and we allow it because we are looking for something to keep our minds off our own problems, or our lives seem so boring, and the drama keeps things interesting.

Everything that comes to us is a reflection of what we put out to the world. Positive attracts positive and negative attracts negative. Gossip a lot, and that negative energy not only comes back to you, it blocks you from receiving good or positive energy. If drama is always around your own life, then start taking a look at what you put out to the universe. Are you a positive-thinking person or negative? Be absolutely truthful with yourself. You may be seeing only what you want to see in your life. How do you think about others and treat them? Do you judge others or gossip? Are you thankful for what you have, or do you think the grass is always greener on the other side of the fence?

This is a good place to start being totally truthful with yourself. You may be surprised what you find. Sometimes we don't even realize that we are being negative. Sometimes we notice something negative about someone else and we actually do the same thing they do and don't even realize it until we are honest about who we are. If you are absolutely truthful about who you are, what you do, and what you have done, and you are willing to change any negativities, your life will change and become more joyful.

It can be hard to look at yourself and be totally honest. While being honest with yourself, don't judge yourself; everyone has things they could work on and change for the better. We are all human, and we all make mistakes. Remember, everyone will grow and learn at their own pace, so don't feel that you have fallen behind. It is your journey and no one else's. It is pretty cool, though, if you choose to make your life better and more joyful.

Working on Myself

I continue to work on myself, and it is truly freeing. It has given me more happiness and joy. I ask my angels and guardians every day to help guide and support me. They are a part of my life every day, and I am so thankful for being able to communicate with them.

When you learn who you are and what you are all about, you may find that some people in your life don't fit in as well anymore. You may find that you don't call them as much, or maybe they don't call you as often. You grow apart, live different lives, and different interests take you separate ways. That doesn't mean they are not good people. It just means that they are on a different path than you, or they are learning at a different pace. You can still be friends, you just may not be as close or see each other as much.

The people who are close to me share the same beliefs and are trying to follow their paths and learn as they go along. I like to have people around me who are positive, have open minds, and want to learn where their mystic highway will take them. As I change, the people around me do, too. They may see that I am happier and want to learn more so they can be happier as well. It could even be that the energy I send out attracts the same kind of people. We do attract the same kind of people, so when we change by finding our true selves, the people in our lives will change.

I have learned that I have only myself to rely on and only myself to do the job that needs to be done to get to where I want to go. I know I can accomplish anything. It is up to me to take the steps and move forward toward the place I want to go. I know where I want to be and how I will get there. I have learned what is true to me and that I need to "be who I be" in order to follow my journey.

I am grateful for all my thoughts, my ideas, and the courage I have had to continue on this journey. I am grateful for all the lessons I have learned, good and bad, throughout my journey. I am grateful for the people in my life and all the support they give me. I am grateful for the guidance and wisdom I have received from my guardian angels, and the knowledge that comes seems to come from out of the blue.

I will challenge myself and the ideas and thoughts that I have to find the answers I need. I will find my way in this life, the way that is right for me, not how society thinks I need to live. Please remember that we are all different and need to find our own way.

I have learned to trust in myself and that I need to remember to have faith always. I am a human being and make mistakes, just like everyone else. And I am also a spiritual being with unlimited possibilities and the power to do anything, just like everyone else.

I am also learning to ask for guidance through meditation. During one meditation, I asked for help because I could never understand why, when I saw my dad, I would talk to him but he didn't talk back, or it seemed like he was trying to but I couldn't hear him. I was frustrated with this and eventually gave up trying. This helped because, as I have learned, when we try too hard to see, hear, or feel the spiritual world, it doesn't work. I needed to relax and allow it to happen and have faith in it. I had to set my ego aside and not listen to negative thoughts. Our egos like to talk us out of things, and it's always negative, so when your thoughts about something are negative, it is most likely your ego talking.

I asked my grandma during a meditation why I had trouble communicating with my dad. She told me that I hadn't truly forgiven him and that I was holding on to negative memories. I realized that I did hang on to those memories, and I needed to forgive and let it go. Dad loved to tease, but sometimes it scared me. I did not like him at all when he would wrap me in a blanket and hold me tight so I couldn't move. I became so claustrophobic from this, and I really needed to let that go. I remembered that he loved me, and he was human, just like we all are. We all make mistakes and do the best that we know how. Just like the French philosopher Pierre Teilhard de Chardin says, "We are not human beings having a spiritual experience; we are spiritual beings having a human experience." Everyone is learning in this lifetime and doing their best in a challenging world.

I forgave my dad, and I gave him a hug. This was the first time since I first started to see him that we actually communicated with each other. He mostly sits quietly in the corner of the room, which at first I didn't understand. But now I know he is my protector and supports me and shows up when I need him, even when I don't expect him. Just seeing him, or any other angel, gives me the feeling of calmness and being safe. This is definitely one of those times of feeling that "knowing" in every cell in my body. He reminds me that I am never alone. He is with me, just like Grandma and all the angels who are with me every day.

I have great gratitude to all my angels, guardians, and guides, which really means that I am grateful to God for all those energies that are sent from him to me. I know this all can be hard to accept, but just think how we are made of energy along with everything else in the world. Our bodies can take on other energies, like radio waves, for instance. Most people can't feel that energy, but that doesn't mean it doesn't exist. So it is interesting how people have a hard time believing in other types of energy.

Our energy flows beyond the universe and is a part of everything. With every heart beat, there is an electrical shock to keep it beating. Our thoughts are energy that flow throughout the world, the universe, or wherever they need to be. Think about the saying, "You could cut the tension with a knife." And now think of a time you walked into a room and you could feel the tension in the room because it was so strong, even though no one told you anything about what was going on. Even at Christmastime, I can feel a huge shift in energy. The energy is amazing and surrounds everything and everyone. It is giving, joyful, peaceful, and exciting all at the same time. There are all kinds of energy around us; we just have to pay attention and acknowledge them. We are infinite energy.

Angel Helpers

It is so cool that when I need a little encouragement or something to get me back on track, the message is always there. I had been feeling unfocused and confused, like I had too many things on my mind that I couldn't sort out. I asked my angels for guidance, and I quickly got my focus back on my book, and everything fell into place. I knew this thought was exactly what I needed to do.

I had a couple of days when I found myself frustrated with my true self-healing work. Then, one morning, I heard Oprah talking about "taking control of your life" and moving forward. She mentioned one time that she had prayed for something and realized that God was waiting for her to take action herself. She needed to take control and take the steps to move forward, but God was also there to help.

I had decided a few years ago that I had to take control of my life and not give my power to anyone else. After making this decision, my life started to change, and I felt empowered by the feeling of having control over my own life. But when I heard Oprah that morning, I realized that a small part of me was waiting for God to just answer my prayers. Even though I had started to take steps toward the things I wanted to happen in my life, I knew I had to turn it up and go for it, and that God would be there for me every step of the way.

There are so many kinds of angels around us. There are all the angels that God sends to us, and the human angels among us on earth. They are the people in our lives who help guide us and give us the words and support we need. Sometimes they are family or friends, and sometimes they are strangers that we meet. They come into our lives when we need them, and they have words or some type of guidance that will help us travel down our mystic highway. We need to live in every moment, pay attention, and listen to everything around us. We continually get messages and support, but we tend to miss so much of it because we are not in the moment. We are racing ahead of time and not truly seeing or hearing what is right in front of us.

I have

- lost my dad.
- lost my nephew.
- lost my grandpa.
- lost my grandma.
- lost many people close to me.
- lost dear friends.
- lost myself.
- lost my way.
- felt misunderstood.
- felt confused.
- felt emptiness.
- felt hurt.
- felt unwanted.
- felt loneliness.
- felt unworthy.
- felt fear.
- felt broken.
- been raped.
- been sexually abused.
- been taken advantage of.
- had depression.
- had many food allergies.
- had physical pain.
- had migraines.
- had fibromyalgia.
- had many struggles.

I have also found

- who I am! I have found what I am about!
- my voice!
- my spirituality!
- my faith!
- my happiness!
- my passion!
- my purpose!
- my way!
- everything I need!
- an *amazing* life!
- *love and joy*!

It may look as though I have more negative "haves" than positive "haves," but that only shows the greater power of the positive "haves." The power of love and of faith are infinite. There are people who have had more unthinkable things happen to them, yet they survive it all by trusting their faith and by letting love, not anger or hate, guide them. I know we all can live happily ever after if we just look at what we have: love, faith, and trust to get us through any hard times.

We all have our own beliefs—God, Buddha, or whichever religion or spirituality you have in your heart. They will all guide you with love. Your guardian angels are always by your side and waiting for you to ask them for help.

I have often wondered why I have gone through so many painful things, and I believe that maybe it was so I would know how others felt, and that would help me understand their pain or situation. I also believe that these things that I experienced were there for me to learn from.

What are your *haves*?

How have these experiences changed you or inspired you?

_____

_____

_____

_____

_____

_____

_____

_____

_____

_____

_____

_____

_____

_____

_____

_____

_____

True Self-Healing

After my first Access Consciousness Bars class, I found that something new was happening when I worked with a massage or cranial client. As I worked, I saw what looked like a three-dimensional mold of the client that hovered over him or her. I had never experienced this before, but I felt comfortable with it. I somehow understood that this was a new modality for healing, and I had to follow it and learn about it. I asked my angels to guide me through this new form of healing. This mold or image is the true self of the client on the table. The mold is what their true mind and body is through God's eyes, how He made them.

The image of the client looked like it was pure energy— billions of molecules energetically moving within the image. I asked for guidance to show me what I needed to do. I felt like I just needed to be the support for this image, and I followed my instincts and asked the image to blend with the client on the table. As soon as I asked, the image started to lower itself and meld with the client.

I found that each mold would meld differently and at different speeds. Sometimes it would start to meld at the client's feet and work its way up. Other times it would start to meld in another area of the body. Each client was different, and the mold for each person melded and healed as it needed.

Sometimes, I found the image would start to meld into the client but would stop at a certain point. This seemed to be a way of showing me a problem area of the body that needed attention. I also got the feeling that the client needed to acknowledge the area and deal with any emotional or physical trauma to that specific area. Because this was so new to me, I didn't discuss these images with clients. I just trusted what was happening and followed my instincts.

I have seen different images. Some seem to be for physical healing, and some images have the feeling of being emotional healers. During a treatment, several images have shown up, one after the other. It seems that after one image has melded with the client, the next one shows up, waiting for its turn. I believe one image can start the healing process, and sometimes you have to work in more than one area to heal a specific injury, and so the next image that shows up will heal another part of the body.

I also believe that multiple images that appear during a treatment can each be for specific things. The first two or three images may be for the physical healing; I see these as energetic cells or molecules. After each image melds, there is a sense of the image settling in, and then the next image is ready to take its place in the body.

The fourth image I see a little differently. It looks like tinier molecules and has a smoky white or hazy look to it. When I see this kind of mold, it feels like emotions, beliefs, or an awareness. Our emotions and beliefs can change our bodies physically, creating pain, disease, allergies, depression, and so much more. We can change all this with our true molds and our way of thinking and by confronting our fears. If we are willing to acknowledge our emotions, fears, and everything else that could be causing problems physically, then we can get rid of the negative energy in our bodies and open up more room for the true mold of us to naturally heal our bodies.

During treatments, I have found that there are a few different molds, and I believe there are more. Sometimes, the mold is the image of the entire body, and sometimes I see an image of a specific part of the body. If it feels right, I will ask for a true mold of just a specific part of the body. This seems to work very well, and the energy is concentrated to one area.

As I watch the true mold meld and start working, I hear a voice say, "Hold it." I know right away that I am to intentionally hold the mold in that place so that it can connect with and "lock" into the body. The mold sometimes needs help to stay in that specific position. I can see the energy or molecules moving or vibrating and attaching to the physical body on the table. If I get distracted and my focus starts wandering, then the true mold starts to move off its "mark" and the healing stops. I then just put my intention back on holding the true mold in the place it wants, and it then continues its healing.

When the true mold is changing the body's physical position, I can physically feel the changes that the true mold is making in the body. It is interesting how I can feel the body twisting and turning, moving around as the cells or molecules move and changing to different positions in order to bring the body back to its normal or true self. While working with a client with scoliosis, I could feel how her body twisted around as it tried to get back to its true self. I could feel the pain move to different areas of the body as the true mold changed the position of the molecules to their true place in the body.

I find it easier to help the healing process when there is no talking during the treatment. I ask questions once in a while, and the client answers, but other than that, I prefer quiet during the session. I can focus on the healing and keep my intentions on track. Then, the energy is more powerful and the healing faster.

Even after the treatment, I find that I still have an energy connection with the client, and I can still use that energy to continue the client's healing. Just feeling the energy, I can change or move it. I can see the client and what is changing for them, and so I can add energy where it needs to be. The power of the thought can manifest itself energetically to the client and help the healing process.

Just like when you think of someone and then all of a sudden they call you on the phone or show up at your door. The power of thought can manifest, and we just chalk it up to coincidence. But the cool thing is that no matter what the excuses are to disprove the theories, the theories are still there, as are the amazing things that the power of energy and the power of thought and the power of our beings still accomplish.

This true self-healing is truly amazing! I am grateful to all my angels for constantly being there for me and my clients.

This morning, as I woke up, I realized that something I have been doing in my massage and cranial work for many years is part of the true self-healing, and I didn't even know it. Quite a while ago—I am not sure exactly when I started doing this or why—I began energetically reaching into clients' bodies and holding the injured tissue or organ, and as I held it, I gave it energy. As I did so, the area would sometimes unwind, pulse, give off heat, shift or move, or whatever else it needed to do. Sometimes, two or more of these things would happen at the same time. I could see my hands hold on to the tissue, and I asked God to send his white light to help it heal. Mostly, I would just hold on and wait for the tissue to do what it needed to do, but sometimes I guided the tissue energetically to give it a little nudge, which helped it to shift and release. It was something that I just played with, and it seemed pretty cool to do. This is what I feel when I am working: energy, hold on, move, shift … time change … feels like time has changed. The energy, cells, or tissue has shifted time. It is hard to explain, but when I feel it, I know exactly what it is. When the tissue changes to its true self, it is in a different time.

During treatments, I also started to notice different colors around the true self mold and the client. These colors are the auras of the angels who are helping and guiding us. Each color is the aura of an archangel, and this gives me guidance to what the problem is and what the client needs to work on—a specific problem emotionally or physically. The archangel with a client during treatment is helping that client heal that area or situation that is keeping the client's true self from melding with his or her earthly being. If you have blocks within your body, whether emotionally or physically, then your true mold won't meld into the body. When you release these blocks, your true self can meld, and your earthly being becomes more of the true being that you are. More than one archangel may come to help during the treatment, and each one is there for a specific reason.

We know that God can heal anything, and we have seen and heard of miracles that happen around the world all the time. So give yourself a chance to have your angels and the archangels help you find your true self. Follow your instincts toward what you need emotionally and physically; your inner wisdom knows what you need to "be who you be." Trust in your thoughts and the ideas that come from your thoughts. They are your thoughts and you know what you need to do. The more you listen and trust in your inner wisdom, the stronger that intuition becomes. As your intuition grows, you will know better the guidance of your angels.

All we need to do is ask our angels to help us in whatever area of our lives, and they will be there for us. We have free will, and our angels will wait until we ask for their help. They are always there for us but won't intervene unless we ask them to. We need to be responsible for our own lives and ask for help when we need it. It is okay to need help, whether it is from family, friends, professionals, or our angels. We just don't want to give our lives to others or expect others to fix our lives.

We tend to abuse our bodies. Our bodies are worked hard, neglected, judged, hated, disliked, ignored, stressed, and forgotten. We rarely celebrate our bodies. We need to take care of our bodies, enjoy, love, be grateful for them, and we should be proud of our bodies. We are infinite! We are energy, and we have the power to make or break our bodies. Our true molds can help change and heal us in every way.

This is why it is so important to be totally honest with yourself. If you can't be honest with yourself about everything, then changing and healing becomes more difficult. Remember that you shouldn't judge yourself, because we all are human and make mistakes. It is just cool when we can acknowledge our mistakes and learn and grow from them.

From emotional or physical traumas to our ultimate purpose in life, it is all ours to live and learn from, not for others. If you give up control of your life and are hoping that someone else is going to fix it, then you will be left behind on your path while everyone else moves on and enjoys their lives. Take one step at a time toward finding what you need and want in your life, and it will change around in no time at all.

Faith and Trust

Today, I have seen and heard the word *faith* so many times, and it hit me that faith is what I would write about. I am learning that the more I let go and have faith, the more everything will work out just the way it is supposed to. When I let my faith take the lead, I become more aware of instinct and intuition. My inner wisdom guides me to new thoughts, ideas, and realizations about my writing and my energy work. Faith requires trust that God (energy of the universe or whatever or whoever is your truth) is there for me and will take care of all my needs and wants.

I have always trusted everyone, but I have learned over the years to be careful with trusting people since so many of them have hurt me and broken the trust I had in them. It didn't mean that I lost all trust in them; it just changed to a different way of trusting them. Most people would simply stop trusting a person who broke their trust, but that was never a thought of mine. When people break a trust, it doesn't mean they are bad people; they are just learning and figuring out their own stuff, and sometimes that reflects on how they treat others. Maybe they haven't figured out their paths or dealt with their personal problems. They are on their own paths and might be learning about life at a different pace. I have struggled at times with trusting people. Sometimes they were just in my life or wanted to become a "friend" purely for their own benefit, not as true friends. I would continue to go back to the friendships time and time again.

I have learned to understand that we are all taking care of ourselves. What others do is their stuff, not mine, and I just need to move on. When I look back to times I knew I needed to move on from situations or from people in my life, I can see now how it was the right thing to do. It was very difficult at the time, but I knew deep down that it was something that had to be done, and over time, I grew more into who I truly was, and my life changed each time I took the steps to move on. I needed to have faith to get through these times, and faith proved itself over and over again.

When I was first married, we didn't have much, but it never bothered me because somewhere inside I felt like everything was going to be just fine. Struggling with farming for quite a few years was very stressful for my husband, and I would remind him that it always worked out and that we always had enough. Of course, there were things I wanted or would have liked to do and just didn't have the means for, but somewhere inside me I knew we would eventually have the life we wanted. I look back to those times and realize that that feeling of knowing that everything would be okay was my faith in God, and he was there for us. At the time, it never dawned on me that the feeling of knowing was my faith. Our inner wisdom is the faith and guidance of a greater power. I call that power God.

Writing about faith reminds me of the poem "Footprints in the Sand." This poem tells us how God will always walk by our side until our dark or troubled times, and then he will carry us. I still remember the very first time I read that poem. It sank deep into my heart. I still remember the feeling that washed over me as I read every word. If there is ever anything that touches your heart when you read it, or a picture that you see, then keep it close to you somewhere you will see it every day so you can be reminded of the feeling it gives you. When we keep positive thoughts, our lives change in wonderful ways. These little things can bring happiness to us, and when we are happier, the people around us change, too.

Having faith will only make life better and way easier! With my faith, my life has changed dramatically, and I have never been so happy. For so many years, I was content with life the way it was. I was happy, but I never truly felt the joy in happiness, that feeling of excitement that flows through your whole body. I knew that some part was always missing, and I really wanted to have that feeling again. I knew I had many things to overcome and work on, but I also knew that joy was there; I just had to choose to go after it. I would talk to God and ask for his help, and the process went from there. I had faith that God would help me, and I just had to be patient and heal myself.

It wasn't always easy to have faith, especially when something bad happened. There was a time when I really didn't like God because I couldn't understand why all these bad things were happening. It was one bad thing after another. I had nothing but faith, and I constantly reminded myself that God would never give me more than I could handle and that I knew I would get through everything I was dealing with. I knew there was light after the darkness, and I would come through just fine. I just needed to keep moving forward, taking one step at a time to get through it all. Sometimes it is easier to just sit idly in the negative thoughts, wondering why bad things happen to us. We end up stuck, not healing or dealing with our problems.

But our lives are worth the fight. We all deserve to be happy and to have the life that we want.

I have learned so very much over the years, and it all has made my life so joyful! My husband and I have changed our way of thinking and of looking at situations, people, and our own lives. The more we have let go and have had faith that we will always be taken care of, the more joy comes into our lives. As I let go and gave my worries to God, I found I was happier than I had been in a long time. The harder you chase after something, like a friendship or success, the faster it runs away. We can go after those things we want by being ourselves, by letting go of the worries and ego-based ideas, like the idea that we can't attain them or that we don't deserve them, and just know that all is taken care of and will happen when it is supposed to. Our businesses are doing better than we could have ever imagined. We have been able to buy our little cabin at our most favorite lake. It is the most peaceful, beautiful place that we could have hoped for. It is like going home every time we go. We are very grateful to God for such a beautiful place.

What is the worst that could happen if you just have faith? The more faith you have, the easier life becomes. So why not try and see what happens? Trust your instincts and follow what is right for you. Trust that you have the answers you need within you. You just need to listen to your thoughts and ideas. These are what your guardian angels or the energy of the universe is giving you. For years, my angels were telling me to write a book, and I always denied the thought. I thought it was crazy, and I had no idea why I kept having the same thought. Well here I am, years later, writing a book!

When I finally made the decision to write the book, I didn't know exactly what it was supposed to be about. Then I heard the words clear and loud: "Write what you know." And I just started to write. I trusted in what I heard and what my angels were telling me, and I knew it was right. I also trusted my angels when they said they would help guide me through writing the book, and I gave them my total faith. When I read about a lecture for "Writing from your Soul," I knew instantly that that was what I was doing, writing from my soul. I knew that I had to go to the lectures! I not only met wonderful people there, but I also learned so much. I learned how the publishing world works and what is expected from us, the writers. I was inspired by the guest speakers Nancy Levin, Doreen Virtue, and of course Wayne Dyer. Every word that Wayne Dyer spoke felt so real and full of love. His energy, his soul, touched everyone in that room. I will never forget the experience.

When you feel something strongly or are passionate about something, then that is what is right for you. It is something you should follow and watch where it takes you. Sometimes it may not seem like it is something you would do, but don't be afraid to try something new. It may just change your life.

I am actually enjoying writing, even though it can be long days, days of feeling off and trying to get focused, or days of reading what I have written and adding words or sentences here and there. I am excited to be writing this book and to find where it takes me. It feels like it will be an exciting journey, and I can hardly wait! I have faith that it will all work out the way it is supposed to, and I will have faith throughout my journey.

Time and Space

Time is such a burden for people. They are racing the clock and not enjoying the life that is right in front of them. Not enough time for their work day. Not enough time for errands and running children around to all the activities. Not enough time for a decent vacation. Not enough time for family and friends. Where do you find the time that has gone by? We try to work or get things done faster to try to catch up and have time, but we only lose that time.

Why not slow down and enjoy the time that is here and now at this moment? Take a breath and just look at who and what is around you. Human reality runs on a clock, and we sometimes have to follow that clock, but don't forget to take the time for yourself. Make a choice to change your life so that you don't have to chase a clock. Live in the moment, your moment. It is when you take those moments that you will find yourself, your happiness, and your way in life. You will see yourself, family, friends, life in all forms, and time differently. Time won't be in control of your life; you will. Watch how differently you see people and the world and how life doesn't have to be as difficult as we sometimes think it is. You will see what is truly important to you.

Time is an interesting concept. I think it holds everything and nothing at the same time. It is now and then, at the same time. Time is man-made. Does it begin and does it end? I think it is one moment all at once. It is a frame of mind, a matter of thought. Time shows itself through day turning to night, but is it actually time? Can we change time to fit our needs? Can we stop time? If time is a matter of thought, can we change time with thought? There is something about time that is very intriguing, mystical— almost like it isn't there. I believe we will see the answers the more we know about the energy of who we are and how that energy is one with all energies.

Our mind and body are in one moment. We learn about time and how it works, but what if there is more about time that no one has discovered yet? I think we should change our thinking about time and be open to new possibilities of how time works. If everything is happening all at the same time, then we should think of what we can do all at the same time or how we can do everything in a single moment. We can do one thing in that one moment, and with thought, we can change or go back in time or hold time in the moment and do something else in that same moment. I feel there is so much more to learn, and the possibilities are endless. What is the feeling or sense of the energy of that specific moment? Find that specific feeling in that moment and you will be able to recall the feeling of that energy and be able to go back or stay in that moment. Do we feel that sense within our soul, within our mind, or both? Do we see the energy field around that one moment?

The senses can trigger memories of times and/or people, like when I hear a certain song and it reminds me of a specific event. Use your senses to see, hear, smell, or feel one moment and then bring it back to each moment. You can feel a shift throughout your body as the energy flows through the body. The shift feels like a quick shockwave that starts around the heart and moves outward throughout the body. The time on the clock continues, because that is how it is mechanically made, but somewhere in us and in the energy around us, we are brought back to that one moment we recalled.

Albert Einstein said, "The true sign of intelligence is not knowledge but imagination." He also said, "Logic will take you from A to B. Imagination will take you everywhere." We have great power within our mind, and imagination will help us find the secrets it holds. Imagine holding time or slowing it down so that you could enjoy a beautiful sunset a little longer or have a little more time to relax and enjoy family.

The concept of time being now and then simultaneously is like the true self-healing, where the true mold is melding with the human body. The true self (the true mold) is the healthy tissue from a different time (from a time when the tissue was at its healthiest) to heal the injured tissue that is there now. When the healthy tissue melds with the injured tissue, you can feel a shift in time. By holding on to the healthy tissue and allowing it to move where the injured tissue is, the injured tissue moves out of the way ... out of the body. The true mold is energy, and that energy melds with the energy of the human body, and I ask that the angels take away the old energy to be changed back to positive or healthy energy. If I notice the new tissue isn't melding easily, then I know there is an energy in its way, and the client needs to release that energy. It could be an energy from an emotional or physical trauma they are holding on to. Once that energy is released, then the healthy tissue can meld into its place. Being that we are human, our body will need time to process this change.

When we realize how powerful our own mind is and have a better understanding of how to use our energy, then we can start to change how we heal. Our bodies react to the smallest things. Even saying the words, "I am in perfect health," tells our body to start healing. I learned the power of these words from Dr. Wayne Dyer. He said these words to himself during his own healing of cancer.

Time Is in the Mind to Mold

I had seen quotes from Albert Einstein for quite a few years, and I was curious why I all of a sudden had an interest in him. Each time I thought of him or saw something about him, I was intrigued, but for the longest time, I didn't take the steps to find out more about him or to explore why I felt that I had some type of connection with him. I was never that interested in science in school, and I really didn't know anything about the man or understand his work. As I look back to all the different times that his name, quotes, or work showed up in my life, I realize now that it was something I needed to research more.

As I began writing about time, I thought of Albert Einstein, and then it hit me that there is some kind of connection to what I was writing. I began reading about him, and though I still didn't really understand his work, when he talked about space-time, I felt there was something familiar there.

I wonder if Albert Einstein and his theories of relativity and space-time have a connection to changing time in thought or through healing work. Time and space are contained in the same path; they have the same journey or pathway. Space gives way to time ... space gives way for the energy which we call *time*. The energy is sent from space to space or lingers in one space. With thought, we can move this energy from one space to another. This energy holds the memories of a time, and we can shift that memory or energy to another space. When we remember a specific time, such as a time during childhood when we played in the park, that thought is an energy, and because it is an energy, we can move it in our thought to another space.

A quote from Albert Einstein: "When you are courting a nice girl, an hour seems like a second. When you sit on a red-hot cinder, a second seems like an hour. That's relativity." How cool that our perception of time can feel so different from the actual.

Albert talks about time and how the faster you travel, the slower time is, and how time is different on Earth than it is in space, such as around a black hole. Now I look at time as an energy within our thoughts and how and where that energy goes from our mind. It starts as a thought, and that energy is sent to another space or place, either to the outside world or to another space within our minds. Whether you are thinking of someone who is right beside you or someone across the country, that thought energy is sent to that person. The energy is received by them, but mostly we don't recognize the energies around us. Sometimes we think of someone, and then all of a sudden they call or just show up. They felt the energy that we were sending to them by thinking about them at that time. This thought energy also travels throughout the universe, and I believe it is received by God, Buddha, the power of the universe, whatever is true to you. So this energy is shifted or moved from one space to another space.

Now the thoughts of your memories are in a space, and when you recall the memories, you again shift the energy of that memory to another space as you think about that memory.

Another kind of memory is from past lives. Have you ever experienced a memory from a past life? If we can recall our memories, then we can shift the energies of the memories of past lives into a space in our present so that we can recall the memories of past lives.

The power of thought can change us mentally and physically. Having the thought or feeling of being younger than you are can change your body physically. People say all the time that in their minds they don't feel as old as their physical bodies are. They age or have aged even more depending on how they have taken care of their bodies. They feel younger than they are, but they need to use those feelings and send them inward to all the cells in their bodies and know that it will change them physically, and they need to take care of their bodies, too.

I think we need to believe that everything is possible so that we are open to the incredible ways that our bodies can change and heal. God has given us all the wisdom we need, so we just have to have faith and follow our instincts. If there is no faith, trust, or believing, then the healing either won't work or will only go so far. When I work with clients, it is the same thing. If they don't believe in what I do or that the power of healing the body is true, then the effects of the treatment are diminished. All I ask is to have an open mind and have faith that everything is possible. What's the worst that could happen? Trust that God has given us amazing human bodies that are capable of so much more than we can imagine.

Our guardian angels send messages, which are energy, to us. We recognize their message as a thought.

We can hear their voices, which is energy. We can get ideas or images in our minds, which are all energies. God, heaven, and his angels are in the space and time that surrounds us. This space and time envelops everything and everyone. It is the infinite energy of all things.

I believe that time is unending—nothing, yet it seems to be everywhere. Space is where we can change the idea of time. I think that we move time from one space to another. We hold a time in the moment we are in. The space holds only the energy of the physical matter of what we see or know is there. Time is only what we have made up to remember where that physical matter, idea, or memory was or when in our lives that matter was. We just use time to recall that matter and bring it forward to our thought, so it is all energy that we are using and changing from one space to another.

Energy is constantly moving around us, inside and out. If we ignore it, then the energy moves around as usual. But if we are aware and acknowledge the energy, then it can change and become more active or more powerful. By acknowledging our thoughts, we can control the power of that energy. We can use the energy to help us as we need. There are many different energies around us, and we can learn what those energies are and how to use each different one. If we choose to be aware of the energies, then we can utilize the energy for changing our lives, helping Mother Earth, helping heal others, or finding new ideas of life and what it means.

There is energy from the sun, moon, Earth, and light, and energy from the spiritual world, like our angels or the energy from the deity that you believe in. There are the energies from man-made objects, like music, radio waves, or factories that emit energies. There are the energies that we all send outward to the universe that are from our thoughts, emotions, or actions. Some energies are good or positive, and some are negative, so it is important to know the different feelings of each of them. You could have a physical feeling, emotional feeling, or a sense of knowing that the energy is negative or positive. Always ask your guardian angels to help you receive only the positive energy, not the negative energy.

Einstein says that it is all relative, so I understand that everything is relative—people, plants, material things, the earth, all energy … everything. The energy of everything is of one cell changing to form into whatever it is supposed to be. Like the creation of a baby … one cell turns into two and then four, continually adding and forming into a little human being. That first cell holds all the DNA to form the baby. Imagine all the energy within that cell and how infinite it must be to be able to create a human body that is so incredibly complex. So if one cell can hold that much energy, then we should be able to do anything with the energy around us, like travel at any speed and not have the object become heavier or bigger.

When we reach for answers to the hard questions, new ideas, or theories, sometimes we need to see the simplicity of the situation, not make it more complicated than it is. Sometimes we try too hard or reach too far, and maybe the answers are right in front of us, within our inner wisdom. Trusting our instincts and inner wisdom will take us further toward finding the right answers.

Einstein's equation $e=mc^2$ says that when an object travels near the speed of light, c, the mass of the object increases. The object goes faster, but it also gets heavier.

If it were actually able to move at c, the object's mass and energy would both be infinite. So in order for an object to move that fast, it needs more energy for the speed, because the object has more mass and becomes heavier, too. The more energy it holds, the bigger and heavier it becomes.

Einstein says that mass and energy are unified. I think they are, because energy makes up everything. Can we use the energy from the mass of the object to create the energy that is needed to get to the speed of light? If time can change by using the physical speed of travel, then why not change time by changing the speed of thought, or mind travel. We can imagine we are anywhere, so why not move or send that energy of thought out to the universe quickly? Like having a higher vibration within yourself, the higher the energy level, the faster the energy travels. The faster the energy travels, the faster you manifest where you want to be or what you want. The higher vibration can bring you closer to the realm of time that is the moment—the only moment—this moment where all time that happens or has happened is. To be able to be in this one moment would bring the insight of all energy. The high vibration of a person can take them to their higher inner wisdom and a place of awe-inspiring thought and instinct.

Love

When you look back through your life, do you judge your actions or other people's actions? Do you blame yourself or others? We all make choices in life, and we all make mistakes. We are no different than the next guy. Do you focus on the negative, dramatic gossip around you, or do you find the strength to not allow the gossip and drama to rule your life and, instead, find the good in everyone and be someone everyone can look up to? If you can open your heart to give and receive love, then not only will your life change, but everyone around you can change. Love is the most important and most powerful energy!

It is important to try to look at people and situations with love and not to judge. This doesn't necessarily mean that you agree with how some people do things, but you try to see where they are coming from and try to understand why they do what they do. Understanding the situation doesn't mean you condone it or agree with it, but it will give you a new sense of love and how having love in your heart will open you up to a whole new way of looking at life and dealing with everyone and everything that comes into your life. The stresses of life won't seem as stressful, and everything will seem easier to deal with.

We love our children unconditionally. No matter what they do, we love them. With any kind of love that we send out, we are changing the energy around us and that person we show love to. That energy is sent out throughout the universe and will actually help support and heal people and the earth that we call home. So if you have that unconditional love for everyone and everything, then the support and healing would be unimaginably beautiful! Everything living on this earth needs love, including the earth itself.

The energy of love will win over any energy. Love is the ultimate energy. Its strength can withstand anything, and the more we show love and have love, the stronger we become physically and emotionally. We just need to choose love above all else. We need to choose love whether we are at a high or low point in our lives. No matter how stressful life gets, choose love. It will bring out the strength and courage inside you to take control of your life and deal with all your stresses. You will be able to find solutions more easily and deal with your problems quickly without having all the drama that can come from life stresses.

Love is a constant energy that surrounds us, but we don't always pay attention to feeling the energies around us. The more love we have, the more of that energy surrounds us. The stronger it is, the more we can actually feel it. Think about falling in love and how that made you feel. The feeling of love is incredible, and everyone wants the amazing feeling. When we think we have lost that feeling of love, we just need to remember what it felt like and it will come back. Sometimes it needs a little help, and you have to work at the relationship to get it back, but it is worth every second of it.

Even the feeling of loving something has an amazing effect in your life and on others around you. If you are passionate about your job and love getting up every day to go to work, that's another way to give the energy of love to the world. It is important to find what you love to do, because it doesn't just make your life amazing, it contributes to everyone and everything on earth. The love of your pets, the love of your hobbies, the love of collecting things, or the love of being outdoors and enjoying nature— whatever the love is for just contributes more love to the world.

Magic and Miracles

Magic is an illusion that our earthly mind believes is an illusion, but our true self mind—our inner wisdom—knows the power that magic has. There is the type of "magic" that is performed on stage by the magician to entertain our earthly minds. And then there is the magic of our inner wisdom, which some people have recalled or found within themselves. This magic is a part of our God-given right, which is the power of the universal energy that we are made of. With this energy, we can do amazing things, and the power we have is infinite.

Magic is a word that is mysterious, powerful, exciting, intriguing, and for some a little scary. If you fear something, then you probably don't know a lot about it. It is usually the fear of the unknown that limits us from becoming open-minded and learning about subjects and situations. The more we overcome our fears, the more we will learn and be able to decide what is true to us. Think of the magic within us as the energy that we are made of and how we can use that energy.

Consider the biblical story of Jesus's crucifixion and how he rose again. He was placed in a tomb that was sealed with a huge boulder, and then Jesus disappeared from his resting place, like magic. God is energy and can move mountains if he so chooses. Moses parted the Red Sea, and it was like magic, but it wasn't magic. It was divine energy, and that energy is hard to humanly conceive. The divine energy is from God, and as humans, we can understand the word *magic* more easily than *divine energy*. I think we see God's magic as an illusion rather than the work of the divine. How did Moses use the energy or the knowledge of energy that God gave him to accomplish this? His faith and courage to believe what could be done caused it to be done. His faith gave him access to his true abilities. Biblically or scientifically, magical things have happened. It all depends on how you look at magic and what it means to you. To me, it is magical how a tiny simple seed can grow to be a magnificent oak tree, or how we can use our energy or the energy around us to do what we need, such as healing the human body.

Many magical things have happened throughout history, and some may be looked at as miracles. It is a miracle when someone overcomes an illness or accident that was said to be fatal. It happens every day.

I read *Dying to Be Me* by Anita Moorjani. This was her journey through cancer and near death to actually healing from the cancer. Her doctors had no answers for her recovery. It is a beautiful story that I will always keep with me. I believe that it was also a miracle that my nephew lived for three-and-a-half years with blood that never went through the liver. Without this process, his blood was not detoxified or given the nutrients, minerals, or anything that the liver provides. Yes, he passed away, but we were lucky to have had him in our lives for three-and-a-half years. It could have been much less. The more we start to believe in the divine God, the power of the universe, or the deity that is true to you, the more miracles we will see around us. Humans, the earth, and life itself will become more in tune and in sync with every living thing.

Forgiving

I always knew that forgiving was a very important part of life, but I struggled with truly forgiving people who had hurt me. There were times I thought I had forgiven someone, but when I was absolutely truthful to myself, I realized that I hadn't really forgiven them. I didn't really understand how to forgive someone, but I always tried.

I have learned that in order to forgive, I have to have love in my heart and look at the person and why they were the way they were. I couldn't judge them for what they did; I just had to see their side of it. I didn't necessarily ask what caused them to do the things they did. I realized that they probably had things happen to them, or they didn't feel loved, or they had no confidence, or they had so much guilt inside them, or they simply didn't like themselves for whatever reason. Or maybe that was just the way they were. All these things and more can lead a person to not treat others with love and respect.

By forgiving them, I wasn't condoning their actions, but it allowed me to release the toxic energy that I was holding on to. That type of toxic energy holds us back from moving forward, learning, and receiving good positive energy. Sometimes, people forget to look at the other side of the situation, which could give great insight into why people do what they do.

People make mistakes or don't know how to treat people right, but that doesn't make them horrible people. When we look at the other side of (look through their eyes at) the situation, we are not making excuses for their actions, but we can see how hard life has been for them such that they didn't know how to deal with their problems. They react to people the only way they know how.

Now, when we see their side of things, we can forgive them and release all the negative energy we have been holding on to. We are not condoning or agreeing with what they have done. We are forgiving them and getting our power back, releasing the energy that weighs heavy on us and holds us back from being our true selves and knowing what true love is.

Knowing When You Need Something

So often I see people dismiss, put down, dislike, or disbelieve in something they actually need in their lives. I have seen people who dislike religion and who won't learn anything about it, using the excuse that it is too much and that they don't want to be forced into it. I really don't think anyone is forcing them to like or believe it. Maybe they are just too scared to look into themselves and be truthful to themselves about who they are. I was taught to believe in God, which I still obviously do, but now I also believe there is more to God than being just one religion. I have a feeling within me that God, the universe, and all that is energy is so much bigger than we know. It is not just what our religion, families, and society have taught us. What are your beliefs?

If there is nothing to open your mind to new things, then you tend to stay in your own little world and pretend everything is okay. That is a very small world with not a lot of true joy. Take a breath, relax, and just listen to something new; it just might surprise you. You may keep your opinion about what was told to you, but something there may open a door for you to learn something new or different. It may enlighten your beliefs. It never hurts to learn new ideas. Doing so may change, expand, or strengthen your beliefs.

What can you lose from being open-minded and learning? Nothing. It is still and always will be your choice about what is right for you and what you believe in. Take a moment to listen and learn something from another point of view, and make your own decision about your beliefs. Just because you grew up learning something one way doesn't mean it is the only truth or the whole truth.

I believe everyone should try to be open-minded to learning and accepting ideas, even if they don't understand them.

I am sure many people research the different energies and what they are capable of. Scientists research energy, like gravity or sound waves and how they work, so why is it hard for some to believe in spiritual energy, angel energy, or any energy-related phenomenon? Scientists have been researching how the world works, changing the way we learn, understand the world, and live in this world. Scientists have changed our world through their theories and discoveries. And if scientists did not question other scientists on their ideas, would they have come as far as they have? If they are questioned on their theory, it pushes them to prove their theory.

Some people, scientists and nonscientists alike, don't believe at all in the spiritual energies or anything related to them. If they can have faith in science and continually explore how everything works, then why not give these energies a chance? Why not be open to the possibilities of what and how these energies work? I believe everything is possible and that we are just beginning to understand the infinite beings we are.

I try to listen to all my thoughts and ideas, but sometimes I find that a thought can get away from me. I am learning to recognize the thoughts and how they are related to me and my work.

Higher Vibration and Time

The intention of believing or having faith in a thought is an energy, and if you combine that energy with the energy of that thought (say the thought is about time and space), it will change the vibration of the energies and become a new energy, or it will change the way you see the thought. The energy it becomes can open your mind to another level. So if you are working on a theory about time and space and you have faith in your theory and the intention of the theory working (or at least learning something new about time and space), then the energy from that faith and intention will create an energy vibration that will open your mind more. And as you see more possibilities about time and space, that adds to the energy, which creates a higher vibration.

The higher the vibration, the more we are open to learning. We need to listen to our instincts and hear and see what our minds show us. If we are open to all possibilities, we are more open-minded, which allows more information in. The more open-minded we are, the higher the energy vibration and the more levels our mind is opened to. The more faith and trust we have, the higher the vibration.

If we want to try and change time through thought (moving a time from one space to another), then we need to bring our energy vibration up very high. I wonder if this is the same concept as traveling fast enough in space to change time. If you need the speed of light to change time, then we need to have a higher vibration. We are speeding up the energy within us so that we can move time from one space to another.

I believe we need to have the energy of faith, the energy of our intention, and the energy of the theory that we create in order to raise our energy vibration.

The higher the vibration, the easier it is to connect to the energies of the spiritual world. The higher vibration has to come from the energy of positive thinking, which is faith, positive intentions, and love—the most positive and powerful energy. To change or move time, does the vibration have to be higher than the vibration that connects us to the spiritual world, by adding other energies? Or is it the same energy vibration but maybe on a different level? Do I need to find the levels (or planes) that this higher vibration moves to and from? As I write this, I have a feeling of being cautious, like I need to be careful how far I take this theory. Yet it feels exciting at the same time. These are my thoughts, and it is okay to explore different ideas.

According to an article about Albert Einstein written by Stephen Hawking, in order to time-travel, you need to travel at the speed of light, but the spaceship you would be in would get bigger and bigger the nearer it got to the speed of light. It would take an infinite amount of power to accelerate past the speed of light. So I say that since everything is energy and we are energy, infinite energy, then we have the infinite power to move time. We just have to learn how to use our own energy.

I am amazed how, every day that I write, I am guided to the thoughts and words that I write. I know that if I didn't have an open mind to all possibilities, I would not have all the ideas and thoughts that have come to me. I know that this is very important and will help me find the answers I am looking for. I didn't know about Albert Einstein's or Stephen Hawking's work, other than they were very successful scientists, and I was pleasantly surprised that my thoughts of time and space were something these men and many others work on, too. I would have thoughts about the two scientists and didn't know why they would pop into my mind until I listened to the thoughts and finally read about the men. It was a great affirmation to me that I was on the right track, and that I should continue following my instincts and thoughts. I believe there is so much about our energy and the power of our energy that we haven't yet discovered.

Back to achieving a higher vibration: I believe we also need to release all the negative energies that we hold on to. The negative energies from injuries, abuses, relationships, guilt, lack of forgiveness, regret, judgment, or whatever has created the negative energies.

As I mentioned earlier in the book, we need to let go and release these negative energies so that we can find joy, happiness, who we truly are, and what our life purpose is. The more we release the negative energy, the more room there is for positive energy. The more positive energy, the more joy and happiness we have, which raises our energy vibration, since the positive energies are a much higher vibration.

Water

Energy from oceans, seas, lakes, rivers, waterfalls ...
  Water has energy that I don't fully understand except that it has such a strong presence. We need water to survive as human beings, but the energy of water calls out to us as spiritual beings, too. The spiritual being is different from the earthly being. There is energy that makes up the physical body, and then there is a different energy that makes up our spiritual being. The spiritual energy is who we are. Our souls and the energy that is our physical being is in every cell in our body that makes a complete physical being.

  How do the two energies work together? Where does the energy of our thoughts play into it? The energy from our thoughts comes from the physical mind and also from the spiritual realm. This is a unique energy because it is born in two different levels or planes of the human and spiritual being. Now I think there are three different energies that work together: physical energy, spiritual energy, and the energy from our thoughts.

  This idea of these energies came from the thought of the energy of the ocean and water. So what does the energy of the ocean have in common with the energies of who we are? Does the energy from all the oceans, seas, and lakes feed our energy or take away negative energy? Does it cleanse away all the negative energies from all living things?

The energy of water feeds us physically to keep our earthly beings alive, and it feeds our spiritual being, giving us the energy to have a higher vibration. That is why we feel a need to be near water, whether it is an ocean or river or lake. I see water as mystically giving us energy, and mostly we don't even pay attention to it. We just have a feeling of wanting to be near it. There is a calmness and serenity that comes from watching and hearing the sound of water.

What about all the living things in the waters? How do they work with our energy and the energy of our planet? These beautiful energies give their energy to us and the planet, and they do it unconditionally. We need to try to live more eco-friendly and stop dumping all kinds of wastes into our oceans, into our water systems, and onto our earth. All animals give without expecting anything in return, and that is why we need to help protect their world, too—not only the living things and beings in the waters, but also the living things and beings on land. Without them, we as human beings won't have a planet to live on.

D. H. Lawrence is an English novelist who once said, "I never saw a wild thing sorry for itself." How amazing is that? All living creatures except humans live a life of giving and love, expecting nothing in return. And they don't feel sorry for themselves when something negative happens to them. They just accept what has happened and move on to the next moment. They don't dwell on the negative or hold onto the negative energy; they let it go.

I first saw this quote tattooed on one of my clients and I fell in love with it! It is a truth that we all should remember and live by.

Yoga

I began practicing yoga about fifteen years ago, and it has been a very big part of my life. I have learned about my inner strength, physically and spiritually. Yoga can calm your mind and body. Studies have shown the health benefits of yoga, from lowering your blood pressure to healing injuries faster. There is no end to the physical changes and healing that yoga can do for a body. If you keep yoga in your life, it will be everlasting to your mind, body, and soul.

When I don't take the time to practice yoga, I notice myself not feeling physically or spiritually on track. I feel so much better when I take the time to do yoga. I feel more connected and grounded with the earth and everything around me. I feel light and stronger. Yoga has helped me get through the fibromyalgia and other physically injuries.

Yoga is very spiritual to me, and I find that it helps clear my thinking. When you are grounded, you can think and remember things better. It can help you release traumas that you may be holding on to physically or emotionally. In yoga, you learn to breathe and how powerful your breath is. As I inhale, I guide each breath throughout my body to every cell. I will guide a breath to a specific part of my body if it needs to release and relax. I continue to hold the position and breathe into that specific part until it releases.

DAWNA FLATH

I have found that the longer I practice yoga, the easier and faster the release is.

As we release emotionally and physically, it opens us up to receiving great energy and insight. I am sure there is much more for me to learn about yoga, and I am happy to see where it takes me.

If you find that yoga isn't right for you, there are many different activities that can help keep you healthy, physically and spiritually. If you prefer to be outside, then there are things like hiking, hockey, skating, curling, biking, softball, soccer, swimming, and so many more to choose from. If you prefer indoor activities, you will find many of the outdoor activities are played indoor, too, plus other things, like pilates, dancing, track running, or even tennis. There is something for everyone; you just have to find what you enjoy doing and do it.

Looking for Answers

I have learned that when a situation becomes difficult, I need to let go, to leave it be for a while. The harder I try to solve the problem, the harder it seems and the further away the answer feels. I had been struggling with writing for a few days, and I knew I needed to just relax and listen to my intuition, but I was trying too hard, and it just got further away from me. I finally remembered what I needed to do, and when I made the decision to take a break from writing, I started to hear my inner wisdom. I knew exactly where to start writing, and the words just came to me.

Finding the answers we are looking for doesn't have to be hard. Let go of the fear of not finding the answer and just allow your intuition to guide you. Instead of driving yourself crazy about not knowing the answer, just be in the moment, take some deep breaths, and put your attention on something else. Read a book, clean out the garage, focus on a hobby, or go out with family or friends and have some fun.

When you get your mind off the problem, the answer can come to you much more easily. If you worry over the problem, you need to let those feelings go—so go out and do something fun. Find something that makes you happy and feel joy and that will open up the door for the answers you need. Listen to your intuition and your true feelings and they will guide you.

If you find that your problem is overwhelming, it is okay to ask someone for help. Talk to a friend; sometimes just talking about the problem will give you insight into the answer. You know in your heart what you need, so just listen to your inner wisdom, and don't forget that your intuition will also guide you, so have faith in yourself, too. We all know our own truth and what we need. Be truthful with yourself and have faith that the answers are there.

We don't want to run away from any of our problems. They are a part of our lives, and we learn and grow from them. They are not always easy, but we need to deal with them. Our lives get better when we face them and do what we need to do to get past them. Sometimes people run from their problems or pretend they aren't there. This will only cause more problems down the line. The energy of that problem will sit and fester and can lead to physical and emotional problems. This energy will drag a person down and block them from receiving positive energy.

It may be scary to face some of your problems, but it is worth every bit of energy you put into finding the answers to the problems. You will find that you feel lighter, happier, and prouder of yourself for dealing with the problem rather than hiding from it.

Learning

I have learned many things over the years, and I am still learning. There is so much to learn about myself, the work that I do, and the world around me. I want to keep learning, and the more I do, the more interesting life becomes and the more possibilities that show themselves.

I know that the only limits to learning, and to being open-minded about learning, are the limits I put on myself. I try to catch myself when I am learning something new and I judge it too quickly. I like to step back and give it a chance, see what it is all about, and then follow it if it is true to me. Just because something doesn't make sense right away doesn't mean that it isn't true or right. Even if I find that something isn't true to me, I know that it still may be right and that it just doesn't fit into my beliefs. I think it is important to be open to all possibilities, even if they are not your truths.

When we stop trying to better ourselves and our world, the energy of life becomes still. If you look at how science has changed our lives and our planet, you can see that scientists are helping life move forward by continually learning. I think sometimes the world is moving too fast with technology, but we have to take the positives and the negatives and just figure out how to deal with whatever challenges arise. We can make it through the challenges and enjoy the good things that happen for us.

Like scientists, we need to be continually learning and making life better too. If we set our priorities with learning and making ourselves and the world better at the top, then everything else will fall into place. If we start to change ourselves and how we treat Mother Earth, our lives will start to change, and our dreams and the life we want will be within reach. If we focus only on the material world, our dreams are further away from us.

Yes, there are people whose only priority is materialistic things, and they have all they could want, but do they have true joy? Are the people in their lives truly a part of their lives, or are they just in the background? How happy are they? Is there true love in their lives? What good is having all the material things if you don't have love and joy to appreciate and gratitude for who and what is in your life?

I have learned to deal with physical and emotional traumas in my life, from my childhood to my adult life, and I have learned lessons from it all. I may not have looked for a lesson right away, but eventually I learned that everything happens for a reason and that I would learn those lessons as I grew older. I used to dwell in the thoughts of how terrible a situation was or ask, "why me?" I learned that I was holding on to the negative energy of the situation and giving my power to the other person in the situation. I was putting up a wall against receiving positive energy, and my life was still for a very long time. I learned that was not how I wanted to live anymore and made the choice to take my power back, to deal with the emotions and do what I needed to heal and make myself and my life better.

I know that many people have gone through all sorts of traumas and have made the choice to make their lives the best they can. I have learned from their strength and courage, and I am so grateful for them and for teaching me that there is always hope and a way to get through the darkest times. When I found myself struggling to get through a situation, I would remind myself of all the people out there who have gone through a lot more than I was going through and that they made it through with hope, faith, determination, strength, and a willingness to forgive in order to get their lives and their power back. How incredible these people are. We truly can learn so much from others' experiences.

We can learn from watching our families, friends, or even strangers. Just pay attention to what is going on around you and how you or others react to a situation. We know what is right and wrong, so why do we sometimes make the wrong decision? Sometimes we find it easier to go along with the crowd so that we don't stand out. I have been in situations where someone was talking negative about another person, and I said something to defend them, and then they turned on me. After that, I was scared to defend the other person, but I have learned that it is the right thing to do. I can see that when a person has no self-worth, has no self-confidence, or holds anger within themselves, they feel better about themselves when they put others down.

Every time we don't stand up for what is right, a little piece of us goes away and the negative energy fills that empty place. When bullies get away with their actions, they create more negative energy within their life and leave negative energy surrounding their victim. The more people who stand up for what is right, the more positive energy will be produced and the less the person will bully.

I think the bully holds a lot of negative energy from some circumstance in his or her life, and the only way they know how to interact is to bully. There may be many reasons why they bully, and we need to learn about them. We need to learn about people and understand why they do the things they do, and to have compassion and an open mind when learning about them.

I am learning as I write this book. I am learning more about writing, researching, energy, the energy work I do, trust, faith, the possibilities of everything, and more of who I am and what I can do. Don't stop learning. It will only make you and everyone around you better.

Souls

Our soul is who and what we are, and it is learning and changing every day. I see the soul like a diamond. Diamonds are the hardest, most durable pieces of earth. They have amazing energy and can change and still be the most beautiful things on earth. They are forever. Our souls are like the diamonds of the spiritual world: they shine and sparkle within us. The soul knows the secrets of everything and can withstand anything. The soul is infinite energy. The soul is the beauty of who we are.

Nothing can break the soul. The soul is forever.

The soul is changing every day, even when we are stalled on our journey. The soul will learn from every moment it has on earth. It is who we are, so learn what you can because your soul will move on and bring everything it has learned and grow even more spiritually. Listen to your inner wisdom—your soul. It will guide you with the knowledge it has.

Our souls are united with other souls—spouses, partners, family members, and friends. We have connections with other souls, such as a romantic soul mate, a united love, or when you meet a friend or stranger. There is a connection between the souls, but we don't take time to acknowledge the meeting because we are sometimes too much in the physical world. If you have ever met someone and had a weird or uncomfortable feeling, that is your soul telling you that something is not right, that your soul is not comfortable with his or her soul.

And then there are times when you meet someone and have the feeling of being very comfortable, or you feel like there is a connection or a familiar feeling about this person. This is your soul telling you that it has some sort of connection with his or her soul. It may be a past connection of knowing this soul already, or your soul just knows that this is a soul of importance to know and have in your life.

When you are united with your soul mate or a loved one, remember that you may be together and share your lives, but you also have your own path in life to follow. We need to learn to be united with love of our partner and still follow our individual journeys. When we support each other on our journeys, the united journey with a partner becomes stronger and allows us to "be who we be" and follow our journey.

Learning a Lesson

We all learn lessons in school, in church, and while growing up to adulthood. Some life lessons help us become the people we are, mentally and spiritually. The hardest lessons are the ones that happen through tragedies. Some things in our lives seem to test us or push us to our limits, and we don't know what it is we are supposed to learn. I always told myself through these difficult times that God would never give me more than I could handle. This didn't mean it was easy, but it did give me the faith that I could and would get through anything that came my way. I didn't know right away what the lesson was or how a particular situation would change me, but I did know there was a lesson in every situation, and sometimes I just had to be patient. The lesson would show itself when it was time.

If you don't look for the lesson in all situations, then you miss out on learning more about life and yourself. We need to be open to learning and changing with every lesson. We will learn lessons from positive and negative situations. When we are in a negative situation, it can be hard not to stay in the negative energy, but if we stay in that negative energy, then we miss out on not only the lesson but also healing from that situation. That negative energy changes who we are, in a negative way, if we don't heal from it. We can hold resentment, sadness, hate, or any other negative feeling that can change who we are. If we can find the positive and start learning and healing, then we will change in a positive way. It is not always easy to look for the positive in a negative situation, but just know that there is always something positive and we choose whether or not to look for it.

Lorne and I have one child, Anthony. He was diagnosed with dilated cardiomyopathy (DCM), which scared and stressed us all more than any of us would ever want to deal with. We have a genetic mutation in my family that causes the heart to enlarge so that it cannot work near to its capacity. The women in my family who have dilated cardiomyopathy have been able to control it with medication, but when the men in my family have gotten it, they have all passed on. That is, until just recently, with the help of the VAD pump. My family has lost many men over the years, including my dad, who was only thirty-six when he passed. My son, Anthony, was diagnosed in March of 2015, when he was twenty-two years old.

Anthony first spent eleven days in hospital. I kept my faith, but I would catch myself staying in the energy of stress and worry. I had to remind myself to give that stress and worry to God, and when I did, I felt stronger and more able to deal with what was going on. I felt grounded and could be strong for my son. There is a lesson to learn for each of us, and I am sure my lesson was to realize how strong my faith was. There may be more lessons for me in this situation, but that was one I knew right away. My husband and son have their own lessons to learn, and I hope I can help them figure them out and make their lives a little easier and more positive.

We knew of a relative in another province who had a VAD pump put into his heart. It kept him alive, and he had a pretty normal life until he got his heart transplant two years later. A VAD is a Ventricular Assisted Device, which is a pump that is attached to the lower part of the left ventricle of the heart and to the aorta. The pump does the work for the left ventricle. I knew the only chance Anthony had was to have the same procedure.

We had some difficulty convincing the doctors that Anthony's condition was genetic and that he would not last very long on his own. The doctors thought a virus had caused his DCM. Anthony was in and out of the hospital and continued to get sicker. By the third week in June, Anthony ended up in the CCU, and the doctor immediately called the heart hospital in the neighboring province. Anthony was air-ambulanced to the heart hospital at the end of June and had surgery on July 13, 2015, to put in the VAD pump.

The surgeon said that Anthony's heart stopped on the way into the surgery, and once they had the VAD pump put in on the left ventricle, his right ventricle had started showing signs of trouble. They had to decide whether they needed to put a right ventricle VAD pump in. They felt it was safe to close his chest, and they kept him sedated for 24 hours in case they needed to do the second surgery. The right side of Anthony's heart began working better, and he didn't need the second pump. Somehow, I knew he would get through the surgery. I learned to be in the moment and feel what my faith was telling me.

Anthony has healed from his surgery, and his life is pretty much back to normal with the VAD pump. He is hoping to have the VAD pump for at least two years before he goes back on the heart transplant list. We are grateful for the technology of the VAD pump and for the surgeons and doctors who took such good care of him.

I have learned to choose to be joyful and to appreciate life and my family even more since my son's diagnosis. I know I do not want to live in fear or worry of what might happen. I want to have joy in my life and work and to have fun with my family. I know that I would miss out on so many fun, positive, and joyful times with them if I chose to stay in the negative energy of stress, fear, and worry. I am thankful for the faith I have because it gives me strength, comfort, an open mind, wisdom, and joy.

We have been on a roller coaster of good days and bad days and days that go back and forth from good to bad all day long. When it is a bad day, we tend to forget the faith we have. I look for my angels and their guidance, and just by talking to them or to God, I find myself feeling better and stronger again. We can find smiles and laughter even on the bad days.

On bad days, you can choose to change the day to a better one, too. Remember: you can talk to your guardian angels any time. They are there waiting for you to ask for help. Find what makes you smile and who and what you are grateful for and watch your day turn around.

Fear

I had been working hard on letting go of my fears, and it was working pretty well until my son got sick. Since then, I have struggled with fear. It is too scary to think of what could happen, and I think about it too much. At the beginning, the fear of losing him consumed me, and I didn't even realize it. When I did realize what was going on, I started praying, talking to my angels, and reminding myself that I had to focus on having faith.

I have faith that he will get through this, but at the same time, the fear sets in and I struggle to keep that faith. When I have a good day of positive thinking and my faith seems to give me hope and happiness in my heart, I think about how everything happens for a reason and how God doesn't give us more than we can handle. It is what it is, and when it is your time to go, it just happens. I am finding it hard to understand that we should have faith and face our fears and let them go, yet I know that if it is time for someone to cross over, then it will happen. So where does that leave me and my faith that God can heal and make miracles happen?

Thinking of all these things makes my head spin, and the fear becomes stronger again. Then I start all over again and tell myself that it will be okay, and I look to my faith to pull me through the fear ... again.

I have struggled with why some people go through physical or mental illness. If God can heal everything, then why are some healed and others not? I have realized that there are so many factors in the answer. One I believe is that every soul has something to learn on this earth, and it just may have something to do with an illness. There are lessons from my son's situation and from my whole family, who has to deal with the genetic dilated cardiomyopathy. Maybe the outcome has something to do with whether we all learn what we need to learn. What lessons does my son need to learn? Maybe this disease is supposed to teach the doctors something, too. Maybe it is as simple as everyone needing to have faith and praying for that wonderful outcome.

We know how powerful prayer is. There have been studies on how prayer can heal. So maybe we just need to learn to trust in the power of love and faith. We just need to let go and give it to God. Sometimes the healing or miracle comes, and sometimes it doesn't, even when we have the faith and the prayers. I have lost many people in my life, and I know they are all in a beautiful place where there are loving, joyful souls who know all the wisdom that we search for here on earth.

It all happens for a reason, and only God knows why at the time. Someday, we will know the reasons for everything. For now, we need to have faith that it all happens when it is meant to happen. We need to realize that we don't always have to have the answers and that everything is working out the way it should.

God doesn't punish us by taking away loved ones. It happens for a reason. Maybe that loved one's soul had learned what it needed to and was ready to go home, whether to God or to the deity of your religion or spiritual place.

I read and look for messages from the angels to guide me through the fear and continually ask them to help me replace the fear with love. I have realized that when I let go of the fear, love or a positive feeling takes its place, and I feel so much better. I just need to remind myself that there is a grand life purpose for everyone and that we need to keep our faith. It will get us through the hard times.

We are human beings with all sorts of emotions, but remember that love and faith are from God and fear and negative emotions are human-made. We have nothing to lose if we let go of fear and allow love to fill the space that fear once occupied.

I will continue to remind myself to let go of the fear and let love in, to keep my faith strong and know that everything is what it is. My spiritual being and my earthly being will be taken care of, along with everyone else. There may be hard times, but with love and faith, we will get through them and be stronger for them. We just need to be willing to learn our lessons, "be who we be," and live our lives with compassion, respect, truth, joy, love, and faith.

I know how devastating it will be if my son goes home to God, and I am trying to let go of my fear of that so that the love of God will take its place. I will continue to pray and have faith that he will get through this.

Maybe that's what life is about: learning to continually have faith and just keep on going. Every time you fall or get knocked down—all the difficult times you face—you just get up and keep on keeping on. No matter what, life will keep going, and we need to keep going, too. This is just how I feel and the ideas of life that come to me and just feel right. This is how I will get through the hard times.

True Self

Spiritually, we are healthy, happy, powerful beings. When we are ill, physically or mentally, as our earthly beings, our spiritual beings are still the healthy and powerful entities that God created. We just have to find our true selves and be able to face whatever it is to become our true selves again. Our true self is within and around us, filling all the space and time of our being.

We have many obstacles to overcome and beliefs to find before we start to see our true selves. We must be willing to set aside our egos, which tell us negative things about ourselves and feed us doubts. When we are able to quiet the ego, we can really start to see all we have been missing and all the possibilities that are there for us.

Our true self is right there waiting to be called forth. We have the choice to "be who we be" and find our true selves. Our true selves start to change at birth, and during our lives, we change and conform to the ideas and ways of the people and world around us. When we keep our spiritual being close to our hearts, then we can hold on to who we are more easily, and our belief in our selves is much more powerful.

There are many ways to hold on to the power of who you are: hold on to your faith and the love within that faith, whichever faith that may be. Be still and listen to your intuition. Don't be afraid of who you are. Live your life in every moment and be thankful for all that you have. Have an open mind to all possibilities. Give yourself everything you need on your life journey, and love who you are while respecting, caring, and loving others for who they are.

Self-healing can come from your true self, your true spiritual being. When you connect with your spiritual being, you may have situations that need to be forgiven or healed before your true self can totally connect and meld into your earthly body. You may have fears, guilt, or other negative feelings and situations that will stop your spiritual self from connecting to your earthly being. As I work with clients, I ask them questions about the energies I feel, and I guide them through these situations so that the true self will meld. Clients need to be honest with themselves in order for the situation to resolve and the true self to meld. Sometimes it takes time because a client has forgotten or hasn't realized that a negative situation has affected them deeply. There may be times when it is too hard for the client to relive a situation, and then we will work directly with the negative energy that is being held in his or her body.

Sometimes we don't know why we are ill or have a disease. Maybe it's because we have allowed stress to control our thoughts. Stress breaks down and weakens the body's ability to fight off illness and disease. I know we learn from everything we go through in life. Learning the lesson we were supposed to and learning who we truly are will help us heal. We all have our time to live and to cross over; it isn't easy to talk about, but it is who we are. When it is our time to go, then it doesn't matter where we are, what we are doing, or whether or not we are ill. It will happen when it is our time.

Sometimes I lose my focus on my faith, like when I become afraid for my son's enlarged heart, but I know I need to always find my way back to my faith. It gives me so much strength to get through the hard times. I pray for him to be healed, and I ask for Archangel Raphael to help in his healing. I have faith in God, and I also have faith that the doctors can do amazing things and that they will also learn from this. I ask my son to have faith and to talk to God and his angels to help give him strength during his illness. I work with Archangel Raphael and other angels during energy work with Anthony. I give him my information and experience, the medical doctors give him their knowledge and experience, and the rest is up to him and God.

My son, my husband, and I laugh as much as we can. Having fun lifts the stress and tension that comes around. Anthony is a lot like my dad: They both love to tease and get a laugh out of you. Laughter is an amazing way to lift your spirits and relieve stress. Even during emotionally hard times, you can find laughter, and it is okay to laugh. Laughter will get you through the hard times and give you strength and a more relaxed body and mind to focus on what you need to do and to hear your guardian angel's guidance through it all.

Simply Simple

When we give our fears and worries away, life really is simple. Simply said, it is what it is, and that's just what we need to realize. We create our own drama for whatever reasons and let our fears and worries take control of our lives. Always running to or away from something, we forget who we are and where we are in life. Life doesn't have to be crazy and dramatic, you just need to choose to be in the moment and choose the positive thoughts.

You will realize that living a simple life doesn't mean it is boring and humdrum. It really is exciting and fun because you won't have the fear and worry holding you back and blocking your way through your journey. Simply let go of the fears and worry and don't judge yourself or others, and you will see how easy life can be. Our spiritual guides, God, Buddha, or the universal energy will always watch over us and guide us through our fears and worry so that we can let them go and simply live our own lives, free from fear, worry, and judgment.

It may seem difficult to simply let go of these things, but if you try to have faith that you will be taken care of and that life will be easier, then you will soon see how truly simple it can be. We use so much energy on our fears that it gets downright exhausting. I have been there and done that many times, and I pull myself out each time and remind myself that that is no way to live. It hurts physically and emotionally, and I eventually get so tired that I give it all up. I just give it to God, and he changes it around for me so that I can get back on track.

When I give away all the fears and worries to God, then life becomes simple again and I have clearer mind, which makes decision making so much easier. I can see situations and people clearly, which makes my life easier. It is easier to see and move away from negative people or situations when they come around. Life falls back into a smooth rhythm and becomes simply happier.

We are humans, and what we learn from infancy on influences who we are and how we live our lives. As humans, we can fall back into old routines, but if we choose to try to step out of that same old way, we will realize how simple it can be and how much happier life can be. We always have our own choices to make in life, and the more we learn, the more and better choices we will have available to change ourselves and our lives for the better.

Simply said, it is what it is, and we move on.

All Is Well

It took me about two months after my son got sick before I started to feel like me again. At the beginning, I was so consumed in worry and stress over the diagnosis that I wasn't leaning on my faith and asking God or my angels to help me. It was like I had forgotten about everything I had learned about my faith and the strength of God and His love. I soon realized that I had to look to my faith to get me through, so I began to remind myself of my faith and trust in the power of prayer. The more I focused on that, the easier things became.

I prayed and talked to God and the angels often. In fact, I did it every day and found my strength again. I asked the angels to guide me in what I needed to do. At first, I wasn't hearing their guidance, but the more I talked to them, the more I heard them again.

I asked God every morning to give me guidance for the day, and one morning, I asked Him to guide me during the day and to give me a clear sign that everything would be okay with my son and all the decisions I needed to make. I got my sign that day, and the same sign showed up many days after that. The words "All is well" were my sign.

I like to use Doreen Virtue's angel cards, which give guidance and inspiration. I asked the archangels for guidance, and in the angel card I read were the words "All is well," and I knew right away that those words were

God's answer to my prayer. That day, I saw the words "All is well" at least three or four more times. The next day, I saw the words again, and after that, I heard a few different people say those same words. Over the time I saw and heard those words, I had that wonderful feeling of God reassuring me that "All is well."

These words were such a comforting and peaceful sign, and they made me smile inside and out every time. I needed those words and the reassurance that I was not alone and that all was well.

My family and I will keep praying that my son will get through this, and that it will be just one of those things in life that we will learn and grow from and that will make us stronger. I am not sure what the future will bring for my son, but I know with every cell in my body and all the energy of my spirit that right now, God says, "All is well."

I know that I need to just keep on going and do what I can and just live life with love and faith. I know it will get me through anything.

Take a Chance and Try Something New

We all tend to get stuck in a rut of routine. Take a moment to think of something you would like to do or to try—dancing lessons, hiking, even volunteering somewhere—whatever you would like to try but have never taken the time to do.

I really enjoy jazz and blues music, but not many around me listen to it. I finally came to the realization that I don't have to have my friends with me to be able to enjoy jazz and blues music. I asked my husband if he would be interested in joining me, and he said he would like to try it. I knew that even if he wasn't interested, I still wanted to go and listen to some amazing blues bands. This was something that I knew I needed to do for me.

My husband and I really enjoyed the first blues club we went to, and we ended up meeting some very good people who became close friends. I am so grateful that we met them and became friends. Just by making that small decision of going to do something that I enjoyed shifted my and my husband's life in a wonderful direction. We had so much fun together and met wonderful people.

My husband enjoys fishing, quadding (on an all-terrain vehicle), snowmobiling, and downhill skiing. I have tried all of them, enjoying some, but not so much for the others. We have supported each other and tried to be there for each other.

When you begin something new, it shifts your life and gives you joy. It is important to take time for ourselves and enjoy something new. Ask your spouse, partner, or friend to join you on your adventure, and then you can try something that they would like to do. Support the people who support your interests. Even if you don't have someone to join you, try it anyway, and you will find new friends with the same interests. Our lives can shift emotionally by giving us self-confidence, self-worth, and courage to do and be anything. Our lives can shift outwardly, changing our energy and attracting more people with the same beliefs, goals, and interests as us.

It is very exciting to know that such a small decision can make a world of difference in our lives. Even taking small steps helps us get to the place we want to be in our lives. Just take a moment to find the things in life that you want to try.

So don't be shy; just try. You never know who you might meet or what you may find, like a new hobby or a new career. If you find something you love and are passionate about, you might find a career or life purpose in that.

Intentions

Your intentions are a powerful way to manifest what you want in your life. Intentions will attract the things, people, or situations that come into your life, so you want to be careful what your intentions are.

I used to be okay with where I was in my life, and my intentions reflected that. I wasn't really moving forward in life or down my mystic highway. My thoughts kept me in the same place, physically, emotionally, and financially.

When I began changing my way of thinking and my intentions for my life in all areas, things began to shift and my life began to change. I set my intentions to expecting more from myself. I would try to live my life rather than just sitting back and watching it pass by. I also set my intentions to wanting more out of my life in all ways, from being more physically active to working on myself emotionally. My intentions about finances changed to knowing that I want and deserve to be financially secure.

It would be nice if things changed right away, but it usually takes time as everything in your life changes. Your intentions will create small changes throughout your life, and the changes that do occur can catch you by surprise. You can start by journaling, being grateful for the people and things in your life, or maybe just thinking positively about everything. You will start to see how your life is changing and how your intentions and thoughts are creating this change.

Your intentions should come from your true self, to "be who you be," not from an idea of someone else's life.

Your Joy in Life

There are many ways to define your life, but the most important way is to know that you are truly you and that you do your best to be the kind of person others will look up to. You can't always please everyone, but by being your true self, others will see your truth. I have faith that they will learn from you and soon realize how important it is to be real and that it is okay that not everyone has the same beliefs and ideas. The only beliefs that I don't agree with are anger- or fear-based. Terrorism is based on fear, anger, and negative energy, and that isn't what I believe life should be about. Just remember that you have your beliefs, ideas, and opinions in life, and everyone else gets to have theirs. We should respect others and their beliefs and see what we can learn from them. So keep in mind the power of each person, and we can all work, play, and live among all kinds of interesting and fascinating people.

When you have hate and anger in your life, you know inside of you that it is time to find the root of those emotions. Be absolutely truthful with yourself and uncover the reasons you are holding the hate or anger. Admit everything to yourself; to lie to yourself just hurts you and no one else. There isn't a lot of fun and joy in life with those emotions controlling who you are. Look for your true self and find the joy within you again. It is there; you just have to start looking for it and work at getting it back. It is worth all the work you put into it. We all deserve to be happy and have fun, love, and joy in our lives.

Give your fears and worries of the unknown—of yourself and of others—to God and know that you don't need to be afraid of what you might learn about yourself or others and who they are and what they represent. Again, I don't like or condone any anger- or hate-based beliefs, like terrorism, and I won't allow the fear of them to control my life. The majority of us just want to live the lives we want and deserve. Our lives are worth working for and making them the best we can.

Take Charge and Have a Clear Blue Mind

Can you imagine if everyone had a clear blue mind, knowing exactly who and what they are and how they could change their lives and the world we live in? The possibilities are endless, and it is so exciting to know that more and more people are looking for more in life than just going through day after day doing the same routine. People are looking for themselves and what makes them happy, and that is a huge step toward a whole new life.

Just imagine what you could do if you could truly find that energy of a clear blue mind. To be so clear and absolute about who you are and what you want, having no doubt about your purpose in life, would open you up to a whole new world. Imagine that world and all the opportunities it holds for you.

Imagine overcoming struggles in your life, recovering from traumatic events, or breaking free from an inability to be yourself. Imagine the happiness and joy you could find on the other side of the trauma or negativity. People overcome these obstacles every day, and I have overcome my traumas, so I know it is possible for everyone to find their way, too. You just have to choose to work at it and imagine the life you will uncover.

By taking charge of your life, you will find that everything you do will come more easily than you thought was possible. When you keep your power instead of giving it away to others, you will know what you need to do and make the decisions that need to be made in your life. It is your life and your way, so take charge and live the best, most joyful life you can. Listen and learn from others, and then choose your way and your beliefs. Everything in your life is your choice. You can choose to be happy and joyful or sad and angry; it is all up to you to take charge and live your life.

Keep a clear mind and you will be able to see the direction your life is heading. When you become confused, fearful, worried, or any other negative feeling, then your mind is not clear, and you can't see where you are going. You can lose your way. You won't make good decisions, or you'll fall into others' ideas or energy. You need to stay in control of your own life, and if you work on having a clear mind, your life becomes easier and more joyful.

Our blue minds will spiritually guide us through life and keep us on our own mystic highways, moving along and learning what we need to learn at a speed that is right for each of us. The blue mind within us keeps us grounded to the earth, keeps us aware of our spiritual universe, and holds the connection between our earthly being and our spiritual being.

With a clear blue mind, we can do anything or be anything, and everything is possible.

Afterword

The next chapter in my life has begun, and I look forward to seeing where it goes. There are many things I am hoping and praying for during this new chapter. I can feel it will be an incredible, truly amazing experience.

This chapter brings me hope and faith on helping and healing others. I want to bring the awareness of the need to take care of ourselves and to "be who we be" so that we can also take care of Mother Earth and everything living.

If we are willing to try, we can change everything. We can all have the life that we want and deserve; we just have to try to take those steps to move along our mystical highway. Once you take the first steps, you will see how exciting it is to look forward to where your journey will take you.

My journey has taught me so many things along the way, and I am so thankful for all the lessons. They have only made me better, more open-minded, and more willing to see the things that are sometimes hard to believe. I have learned that we need to look at a life and its mysteries exactly the way they are and not put so much worry and thought into them. Sometimes, the harder we try to understand something, the further away the answer becomes. I have been more confident, stronger, and open "to be who I be."

Sometimes, we all need strength to get through difficult times, but in the middle of a crisis, you may find yourself lost in the energy of that crisis. This is where I found myself when my son got sicker and was admitted back into the hospital. Every day, he got worse, and I was lost in it, trying to keep a positive outlook and hope in my heart. This was the hardest part of my whole life's journey, and it would get even scarier.

I just reminded myself every day of all the things in my life to be grateful for, and that faith gave me the strength I needed. We all have great strength within us, and sometimes we just have to remind ourselves that we can get through anything; the strength is there.

I signed on with Balboa Press Publishing just two days before my son went back into the hospital, and so I knew my book would be on hold for a while. I didn't know we would be sent by air ambulance to another province and wouldn't see home for months. It's been over two months, and I'm still away from home, but I am finally okay enough to finish the manuscript.

It feels so good to be back, writing and working on the manuscript. It makes my heart smile.

I give you my heart and soul in this book, and it is now your beginning, so the words in this book will continue. As you read and find your way, you will add your own beliefs, ideas, and wisdom that is your way, your true self. My words are just here to help you find your own words, the way you truthfully and honestly are as a human and spiritual being.

Have faith in yourself and trust your instincts and inner wisdom. The wisdom is within you; you just need to learn to listen and trust what you hear. Imagine the being you are and the life you want. Your imagination can take you anywhere and everywhere.

Be open to new people and new experiences and allow yourself to have fun and joy in your life. Life is exciting, and you never know what is waiting for you when you choose to move forward and make your life the best that you can.

Remember that you are never alone; your angels or spiritual guides are with you always, and there are always people around you who love you even if you haven't met them yet. Maybe they will come into your life as you begin your travels down your mystic highway.

I write from my soul to your soul, and I pray that you find your way down your mystic highway. I give you my thoughts, ideas, and beliefs and hope they will help you find your way a little more easily.

I will strive for a clear blue mind, by being open to all that is possible in the world, the universe, and the spiritual world. I will believe in myself and the power of my spiritual being. I will be crystal clear on what I want in life, in myself, where I am going, and every step to get there. A clear blue mind is where I will find all the answers I am looking for.

Printed in the United States
By Bookmasters